Customizing
CARS

Customizing CARS

COLIN BURNHAM

GODFREY CAVE ASSOCIATES LIMITED

Designed by Anne Baum
Illustrations by David West

© 1980 Blaketon-Hall Limited

First published in Great Britain 1980 by
Godfrey Cave Associates Limited,
42 Bloomsbury Street,
London, WC1B 3QJ.
(Telephone: 01-636 9177)

Colour reproduction by
Kleur Litho, Bexleyheath, Kent.

Printed and bound by
Hazell Watson and Viney Limited,
Aylesbury, Bucks.

ISBN 0 906223 16 4

Contents

In the Beginning...

The interest in customizing, or the art of changing a standard factory-built car into a personalized creation, actually began building momentum shortly after World War II. Thousands of young G.I.'s returned home to the United States in high spirits, ready to buy the car of their dreams and get moving again. The problem was that new cars were scarce and those that were available looked out-dated, style-wise. During the War, technology had made great advancements and everything was being re-designed to reflect the new 'aerodynamic age'. Young men shopping for new cars didn't want something that had been punched from pre-war dies. Instead they bought what was available, usually the semi-rounded Fords of 1939 onwards, and took them to the West Coast metal artists to have them 'customized'. These 'custom shops' were often run by the redundant coachbuilders of the past, while others were started, or converted from standard body repair shops by youthful talent.

Customizing naturally meant making the car more streamlined, smoothing and blending the lines to give a more aerodynamic shape, or at least an illusion of such. 'Mild' customizing would consist of moulding off all unnecessary protuberances such as chrome trim, door handles, headlight and tail-light housings and so forth. Then the car would be lowered as much as possible, usually more at the rear than at the front, and in many cases to the point of impracticality. Fender skirts would be attached to the rear wheel openings and chromed one-piece hubcaps replaced the standard items. The car would then be given a lacquer paint job, and subtle pin-stripes to highlight the favourable features.

Of course, those who had more money to spend and an expert body-man at hand could go much wilder. Extending the rear fenders to make the car longer was popular. Even more so was the blending or taper-ing of the front fenders all the way back to the rears, known as 'fade-aways'. The final logical step in creating a streamlined vehicle was to chop the roof — not only lower it, but to gracefully blend the rear of the roof in a smooth taper to the back of the car.

The innovators, responsible for the creation of many early customs, included such names as George and Sam Barris, Joe Bailon, Dean Jeffries and Gene Winfield. These artisans also helped the sales of many enthusiast magazines that sprung up in the fifties; *Rod and Custom, Honk, Motor Trend,* etc. — all ran regular build-up features on the classic customs. Consequently, the craze spread rapidly across the States and custom shops soon appeared everywhere.

The spread of customizing as a social phenomena was, to a large extent, due to the way ordinary people looked at the cars. Most of the true customs didn't have the souped-up engines of the hot rod set, who gravitated to the earlier body styles like fenderless '32 road-sters and coupes, and were often exhibitionist about their car's performance. The majority of customs had stock engines and any equipment added under the hood was generally for show and sound. Because of this de-emphasis on engine perform-ance and their low ground clear-ance, customs were driven in a slow, careful manner. This meant acceptability to parents, tolerance by police, to say nothing of the guaranteed social success with the 'guys and gals'.

Of course, there were those that ridiculed the dungareed enthusiasts and referred to their cars as 'low and slow' or 'leadsled'. The latter term

achieved respectability as a hobby/ sport and was growing rapidly. Enthusiast magazines devoted more space to engine tweaks and handling as opposed to custom body modifications and songs that were about performance reached the top of the charts.

The leading car manufacturers soon became aware of the commercial possibilities within the trend, and special performance packages known as 'muscle cars' were introduced to appeal to the younger buyer. These cars incorporated big engines, four-speed transmissions, heavy-duty suspension and a distinct 'street racer' look.

The performance trend lasted until about 1972/3, when the U.S. government imposed heavy restrictions on exhaust emission and insurance companies called for lower horsepower. Once again, the lack of excitement in the new factory-built cars stimulated a general return to customizing. Also during the early seventies, the need for personalized transportation crossed the Atlantic to Britain and other parts of Europe, where the craze soon became very popular.

In recent years customizing has taken on new directions. Many enthusiasts have turned to the utilitarian pick-up truck and panel van as a basis for their creative ideas. Easily available accessories, such as wide mag wheels and instant glass fibre customizing kits have, to some extent, determined the 'sleek' contemporary look. This is not to say that the radical, one-off jobs are not still being done. The current interest in fifties nostalgia, brought about through films such as *American Graffiti,* is responsible for the re-birth of many early customs and a return to the 'cruising spirit'. Street rodding (formerly hot rodding) is now a refined automotive sub-culture, enjoyed by thousands of dedicated enthusiasts.

Like the clothes we wear, custom trends may come and go. But one thing is for certain — as long as there are mass-produced cars on the road, the individual spirit of customizing will live on.

had particular justification since many cars carried up to 100-lbs. (45-kgs.) extra weight in lead filler, which was used to fill seams, windshield posts after chopping, and so on. Most of the countless fifties customs spent their lives being washed, polished and displayed at drive-in restaurants, or any other place where a crowd could be assembled.

Commercially organized custom shows soon became a regular occurrence and great prestige was attached to winning one of the coveted awards. This in turn led to intense competition between the entrants and 'chrome and more chrome' soon became the eye-catching order of the day. Many of

the competing show cars became 'all show and no go', where the only limitation was imagination, and available dollars. Some incorporated completely chromed undercarriages and fully upholstered trunks and wheelwells. By the late fifties/early sixties, customizing had come a long way since the days when a simple interior was all that was needed and chrome was thought to be something you took off a car. Eventually, this over-glorification led to the downfall of the low slung fifties custom.

By '62 the cars, clothes, hairstyles and interests of young people had changed. They saw little point in investing big money and effort into something that would be of little practical use. The emphasis switched to high performance, and everybody wanted a jacked-up Chevy or Pontiac. This change in attitude was also due to the fact that drag racing and performance had

Choosing a Theme

The diverse world of customizing is often partially responsible for initial indecision amongst would-be enthusiasts. In some cases, the majority of cars at any major show or event will look very desirable on first sight, though sadly beyond your means in terms of budget and personal capabilities.

First, it must be established that every personalised vehicle is simply a reflection of the requirements and personality of the individual owner. A car that satisfies the needs of one person may, after careful consideration, be totally unsuitable for you. Also, it is a common misconception that endless funds are necessary to create an effective custom. Lack of cash can often be made up for by hard work and initiative, and almost anything is possible with enough determination. Pre-planning is the most important aspect of any successful project, so think carefully before you rush into it.

Street machine

Although the term can be applied to virtually any post '49 personalized vehicle, a street machine is generally built to perform rather than cruise. The basic idea is to modify a car so that it is capable of blowing the doors off the opposition at the boulevard stop light, or at least have an outward appearance of potency.

The street machine movement evolved during the late fifties/early sixties, when a sizeable segment of American auto enthusiasts were being turned on by straight line performance and high-revving dragstrip machinery. Naturally enough, drag fever soon hit the streets. Young guys channelled all their hard earned money and effort into making their emulative, Super Stock drag cars go faster. Standard engines were replaced by compact and powerful small block V8's, which in turn were swopped for big blocks. Performance was upstaged by whatever means possible.

Tyre technology was pretty low at the time, and the only way of reducing wheelspin from a standing drag start was to put as much loading on the rear wheels as possible. Consequently, the back ends of cars, both on and off the strip, were jacked up high and lightweight tube axle arrangements installed at the front. This set-up helped the car to rise under hard acceleration, thus transferring more weight to the back.

During the early sixties, the ultimate street status symbol was a high flying 409 Chevy or a Pontiac GTO, the first factory-built muscle cars. The Detroit auto moguls soon discovered that 'performance sold', and the race for bigger horsepower was on. New 'factory bullits' appeared each year in order to satisfy the ever increasing demands for improved performance. Those with neither the money or inclination to buy a Mustang, Camaro or Hemi-powered Challenger from a dealer's showroom, drove the archetypal hopped-up '55 Chevys, complete with no-nonsense, grey primered panels. At the local hamburger drive-in, conversation meant

compression, carburation and horsepower. Tyre-smokin' street action was neat.

This rapid pace continued until the early seventies, when government restrictions on exhaust emission and sky-high insurance premiums had all but emasculated the Ford, GM and Mopar muscle cars. Nevertheless, despite the Great Smog Crusade and today's fuel problems, the street machine movement is still very much alive and well, albeit in several different guises.

If the strip-inspired theme sounds like your idea of fun, there are basically three ways to go about it. The first, and most obvious, is to buy a genuine sixties muscle car, although this could prove expensive as they are now highly collectable items, and more of an investor's choice than a personalized project basis. The second is to select a full-bodied stocker with enough 'tough potential' to accept readily the traditional treatment. A good bet is something along the styling of the mid-fifties Chevys. Finally, you could always take an unsuspecting vehicle, be it old or new, large or small, home-grown or foreign, and

impose a radical, performance-biased change of character. The street machine scene is one which invites people to do the outrageous.

Guaranteed to send a shiver up the local sheriff's spine, the hiked-up all round street racer look is probably the most radical modification you can technically make. However, in recent years there has been a move away from this set-up, since the ride it produces is not really one of everyday 'streetability'. A slight hike at the back is often just enough to give the mean and purposeful impression. Current drag-emulated trends lean towards stock rear height and a lowered front end, with 'big 'n' little' racing type mag wheels and tyres.

Engine-wise, a heavy V8 is really the only way to go if you want to create a real stormer. If your budget will stretch to it, a chrome-plated 'blower' poking through the hood will more-than-complete the image.

In contrast to the out and out street racers of the sixties, many of today's street machines are made to look as good as they perform, with immaculate paintwork and trick interiors. The quality of finish and detailing that you apply to these areas is something of a personal choice, but one which should not detract too far from the basic essence.

Left: A straight line of muscular street machinery. *Inset:* License plate from a supercharged Chevy. *Top:* This Renault Dauphine started life with a humble 850cc rear engine. *Centre left:* It now carries front end Cadillac V8 'motorvation'. *Centre right:* Under-hood detailing at its finest. *Right:* Cars along the same lines as this tough '55 Chevy hold great potential.

Street rod

The motto of The National Street Rod Association is simply 'fun with old cars', and basically that's what street rodding is all about.

The word 'rodding' has been around since the early thirties, when model 'T' Fords were cheap and plentiful for the younger buyer. After Henry Ford unveiled his famous flathead V8-powered Model 'B' in 1932, 'T's were considered firmly outdated. But, for those seeking low-buck, high performance fun, the natural thing to do was to buy an old 'T' and slip in a 'B' engine.

There were two places for the first hot rodders' to race their souped-up roadsters; on the boulevard or on the circle track. The first was illegal and dangerous, while the second involved racing around a quarter mile dirt oval, and usually spelled disaster for any decent sheet metal.

It wasn't long before rodders' discovered the smooth, concrete-hard dry lakes of Southern California as being the perfect place to test their machinery. Hundreds of cut-down roadsters turned out each weekend for spontaneous straight line racing, often five or six abreast. Obviously, this became as dangerous as racing from stop light to stop light and some sort of organization was needed. Consequently, the SCTA (Southern California Timing Association) was formed in the late thirties to put an air of decency to the whole affair.

During the war years, the Air Force took over the dry lakes and the vast majority were permanently closed to hot rodders. The early fifties saw the birth of the drag strip and a gradual split between race cars and the typical street-driven hot rod; running a flat-head engine bolted in a '32 Ford chassis, with a chopped, black and flamed roadster or coupe body.

Towards the end of the fifties, hot rodding tended to stagnate as the general emphasis switched to customizing and the show circuits. By the mid-sixties, young guys had lost all interest in spending much of

their spare time building rods, and Detroit muscle cars dominated the street scene. That is, until '72, when government restrictions were indirectly responsible for a renewed interest in rodding or, to be more precise, street rodding. A more refined approach to rebuilding early cars (pre '49) resulted, and has developed into a semi-global sport.

Although almost any early car is game for rodding, the late twenties and thirties Ford body styles are still

Top left: An open-engined 'T' bucket, a pair of highboy roadsters and the legendary '32 Model 'B' coupe. *Note* the hot rod louvres. *Centre left:* Chopped and flamed coupe is reminiscent of the early salt lake racers. *Lower left:* Yellow Deuce is straight out of the movie 'American Graffiti'. *Top right:* Radical V12 Jaguar-powered 'T'. This show winner features a home brewed body, frame, headers and so on. *Centre right:* Fun is the name of the game in a pristine Model 'A' Sedan. *Right:* American example of Britain's favourite street rod, the Ford 'Pop' or Anglia. All original steel panels, narrowed rear axle and racing type mags make this four-seater a neat rod.

the most widely used and best loved amongst street rodders. Original examples are obviously very hard to come by and this is the reason for repro-rods being so popular today. There is hardly a single early Ford part that you can't buy in reproduction form, from grille badges to complete glass fibre, or even steel bodies. In other words, it's possible to build a complete ground-up street rod such as a T-bucket, without using a single original Ford part.

Restoring and modifying a car over thirty years old is likely to be a formidable task that could involve months or even years of hard work. In fact, any worthwhile rodding project will require a lot of pre-planning, patience and determination, so think carefully and consider the task from all angles before you rush into it.

The beginning in terms of rod construction means the fundamental structure upon which everything else is attached — the chassis, or frame. The design of your frame and the various mechanical components you bolt to it will determine how your rod handles, the ride it gives and its general comfortability.

Purpose-built rod chassis are available from several specialist firms, ready to accept the popular repro or steel bodies. They are sturdier and more versatile than the originals and can be purchased in various stages of completion, from a basic framework, to 'complete' with independent suspension crossmember and mounts, steering box mounts and so on.

If you decide to build a 'non-standard' Ford street rod, you'll either have to restore, rebuild or otherwise refurbish the original manufacturer's frame, or fabricate a totally new steel tube item, tailored exactly to the requirements of your body and mechanics. The latter is not something to undertake unless you have specialist knowledge in chassis theory and welding. There are literally thousands of possible variations in suspension systems, steering, brakes etc. Therefore, it's advisable to do plenty of research in these areas and shop for different opinions before you start to build. Most important of all, establish how much you can afford to spend and incorporate every component into that budget concept.

Experts have spent years design-

ing systems for automobiles that will work for you in your rod planning, if you integrate them properly within your puzzle. In other words, try to use as many components of the same original system wherever possible, for better compatibility.

Unlike the hot rods of years ago, today's street rods are built with a strong emphasis on comfort and reliability, together with clean, uncluttered looks. Independent suspension set-ups are very popular, particularly Jaguar, since they give a superb ride. Jag front ends are lightweight and attractive, while a chromed and exposed rear end is a thing of beauty. Of course, quality costs money and if your budget doesn't stretch that far you could always go for a conventional live rear axle arrangement with a less prestigious independent front suspension. Alternatively, and for a more purposeful looking lowered front end, a dropped tube beam type front axle/four bar radius rod layout is neat.

Whenever big horsepower engines are swapped for stockers, it's essential to balance the stopping power pro-rata to the going power. A good, efficient braking system is very important. Better rear brakes will come with whatever rear end you install, but always check the components and rebuild as necessary. At the front, go for disc brakes rather than drums as they are more efficient and easier to maintain. If you use different systems at front and rear, the operational pressures must be properly balanced. Also, if you rebuild an early car, always replace the old brake pipes.

Above: Topless rods are great in the summer. *Left:* This 'T' incorporates a dropped tube axle and disc brakes. *Right:* A fully chromed Jag rear end. *Far left:* 'Low Blow'. *Lower left:* Conventional rod interior. *Lower right:* Street rodders cherish their cars.

The steering department is very much a matter of proper blending of total systems. Rack and pinion steering is designed for use with independent front suspension and this combination can be very satisfying. Rack and pinion is not really suited to a beam axle set-up and a conventional steering box/column, such as the adjustable VW bus unit, will be more effective.

Your choice of powerplant will depend on several factors, most notably budget. Initial purchase, cost of rebuild and running costs should all be taken into account, especially the latter with today's escalating fuel prices. Nevertheless, by tradition, a V8 is the only way to go. A mildly modified small block Chevy or Ford, maybe with auto transmission, will certainly produce enough power to make your rod fun to drive. If the engine is to be exposed for all to see, as in a 'T', you can colour match it with the overall colour of the car and adorn it with any number of chromed or polished cosmetic accessories.

Bodywise, the 'state of the art' leans heavily towards a subtle restoration approach, keeping any modifications very subdued. Original (or repro) trim, bumpers, headlights etc. should be kept in place, while a simple, one colour paint job will look most effective in creating the 'genuine' look. Obviously there are no hard and fast rules, and you may wish to chop the roof and add some flames for a real 'hot' street rod appearance.

Interior and upholstery treatments should be of a tasteful, traditional nature and it's a good idea to keep any necessary instrument changes in keeping with the original dashboard. Wire wheels and radial tyres tucked neatly under the fenders will add further authenticity, although wide mags are still very popular.

Summing up, it may seem like a lot of time, money and specialist knowledge is needed for a project of this nature. The fact is that anyone, with enough enthusiasm, initiative and DIY skill, can enjoy the fruits of building and owning a street rod, be it on a low or high budget.

Low rider

Perhaps the most 'personal' of all custom themes is that of the ground-hugging lowrider. Basically, it involves taking an ordinary vehicle and transforming it into a smooth, low-profile street cruiser.

The roots of lowriding go back to the mid-fifties when chopped-top Fords and Mercurys were considered the 'koolest kustoms' around. During the proceeding sixties when the performance trend took over, many of these radical customs were sold for paltry sums on used car lots, or left to rot. In the early seventies, a reaction to the muscle car movement by the young Mexican-American *vato* brought lowriding back in new ways. Late model passenger cars were treated to lowered suspension, wild paint jobs and sumptuous interiors. Add to this ever-growing California cult the general interest in fifties' nostalgia, and you'll see more lowriders, both resurrected and contemporary, on the streets of America today than at any other time before.

If the low look on life appeals to you, a long, round-bodied car from the fifties will do much to reflect the early custom flavour as a basis for your project. That is not to say that the more up-dated pan-scrapers, some of which incorporate sharp angular fins, are any less impressive. Almost any car will look effective given the lowrider treatment.

Firstly, the simplest way of getting the car 'down in the weeds' is to cut the front springs and add lowering blocks at the rear. Alternatively, and

Above: Aircraft hydraulics enables ground level parking for this lavish lowrider. *Left:* A chopped Mercury with flipper hubcaps, lakes pipes, appletons etc. equals one Kool Kustom. *Right:* Clean mid-fifties Oldsmobile incorporates subtle touches. *Lower left:* Fine pin-striping adds class. *Below:* Garish Merc is a real head turner. *Lower right:* Cruisin' the boulevard.

for ultimate status, hydraulic jacks could be installed to raise or lower the car at the flick of a switch. A roof chop will certainly enhance the low image although it is no easy task, especially on the curved body styles of the fifties.

You can achieve a smooth, one-piece look to the body by incorporating many traditional custom tricks. A firm favourite is to remove practically all the exterior trim and fill the resultant holes. Handles and locks on doors and trunk lid can be replaced with concealed, electrically-operated mechanisms. Seams between abutting panels should be filled and smoothed, and headlight/tail-light housings blended into the

front and rear fenders respectively. Recessed, or frenched, license plates, side lights and aerial(s) will also help to produce clean, simple lines. Detachable rear fender skirts are a must, as are skinny, chromed Lakes pipes running beneath the rocker panels. If you find the stock grille undesirable it can be replaced with a chromed tube item, mounted so as to appear floating within its opening.

Traditionally, paint is kept fairly simple, consisting of, say a single or two-tone candy effect and some subtle pinstripes. However, many of the contemporary lowriders are far more conspicuous, incorporating flames, scallops, flake and various other 'glitter' techniques. Similarly with interiors, the styles range from mild to wild. From a basic fifties' tuck'n'roll upholstery job to the womb-like crushed velvet theme, incorporating swivel seats, drinks cabinet and a tiny chain-link steering wheel.

For the true 'nostalgic cruiser' image, standard wheels should be dressed in polished one-piece hub caps and broad whitewall tyres. Alternatively, a set of chromy spokes encircled with a narrow white band will personify the 'sleek' Chicano look.

Needless to say, engine and running gear are normally left stock, since impressionable high speed is of little importance to the street-prowling lowrider.

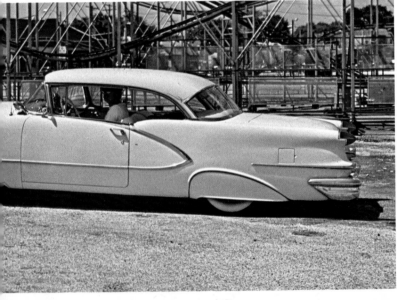

Small van

In addition to being very practical vehicles to own and drive, small vans have great visual potential. They are generally cheap to buy and are well worth considering if you wish to create a street custom with a difference.

Vans were first exploited by the West Coast surfers back in the early sixties. Although a Woody (see glossary of terms) was considered the ultimate surf wagon at the time, they were scarce and much sought after. The next best thing for hauling surf-boards around was a panel truck or sedan delivery, similar to a shooting brake without side rear windows. Almost overnight mid-fifties panels became the 'in thing' all along the California coastal highways. The surfers, and others who saw these vehicles on the streets, soon discovered they were neat for more than just carrying surf-boards. They could not only look sharp and go fast like the typical hot cars of the era, they also included a private little room in the back which was useful for all sorts of things. Tricked-out vans had arrived on the scene.

Nowadays, panel vans are subjected to all types of conversion. From the out and out street racer, complete with every performance trait, to the super slinky, lowriding kerb crawler. Obviously the basic character and shape of the van dictates, to a high degree, the kind of conversion it will readily accept. So, if you decide to take the commercial route, first establish what effect you're after, then set about finding a suitable base vehicle. Don't be restricted by what is easily available or proven vehicle treatments. By starting off with something slightly unusual, you're more likely to end up with an interesting result.

Sedan deliveries hold a lot of appeal as they combine the refinements of a car with the utility value of a van. Old pre-fifties models are becoming increasingly rare, so if you fancy the idea of a 'gennie' street rod delivery, be prepared for a long hard search.

Alternatively, you could always convert an old sedan, or similarly a shooting brake. This would involve removing all of the side rear glass, welding up the side rear doors, and panelling in the resultant gaps with sheet steel. A single, side-opening rear door would also be necessary for true authenticity.

Apart from deliveries, there are, of course, numerous small commercial vehicles of all ages to choose from. Also, the slightly 'alien' character of many old foreign vans can often be used to good effect.

Any enclosed van project provides a chance to be inventive with exterior sheet metal. Murals, lettering and wild paint designs are commonplace on contemporary custom vans. Even the understated rod restoration will benefit given a neat touch of traditional, commercially-orientated lettering.

Top left: An old delivery can make a classy rod.
Above: Flames, murals, lettering, this Ford Anglia has got the lot.
Left: A '56 Chevy 'high-jacker'.
Right: 'Vanpire' — a tasty commercial.
Below: 1940 Ford Delivery — the 'gennie' approach.

Likewise, interiors offer plenty of room for speculation. You could go for the 'luxurious lounger' effect with deep buttoned side panels and headliner, thick pile carpet and a mind-blowing stereo system. In contrast, your thoughts may be more inclined towards the vehicle's performance, in which case the interior would be purely functional, say panelled in aluminium and wood.

As you can see, small vans have a lot to offer both the radical customizer and the enthusiast seeking a fairly 'low-buck' means of fun.

Above: Early Minor 1000 van incorporates V8 power and re-styled one-piece front end.

Pick-up

In stock form, most pick-ups are plain, non-descript vehicles — in other words, they are just the kind of challenge customizers love.

Over the past decade, this basic form of transportation has been subject to much creative treatment, and is now an established automotive cult in the U.S.A. Variations range from subtle re-styling to radical conversions of late model luxury sedans. There are indeed numerous ways in which to exploit the utility value of the pick-up theme, and create a tasteful 'custom hauler'.

You may wish to breathe new life into an old commercial workhorse. If so, it's worth taking the time to search for an example that's in reasonable condition. More often than not they have been hammered to within an inch of death, day in and day out, and will require a full toes to nose rebuild — not a task for the half-hearted. Nevertheless, the dated character of an old pick-up truck will provide a good basis for subtle improvement. This can include an up-dated powertrain, tasteful chrome plating and an elegant paint scheme/interior.

Alternatively, an uninspiring sedan or shooting brake will often look very effective given the pick-up treatment. With a knowledge of sheet metal work and welding techniques, the conversion should present few problems, and by taking this route you can produce a real, one-off custom. As with any radical body chop, it's advisable to sketch out your plans on paper before you attempt the real thing. This way you'll get a good idea of the new identity, and whether or not it will visually accept the styling you have in mind; be it anything from a neat and restrained, purpose-built custom, to a low-riding luxury hauler — the choice of treatment is all yours.

Contemporary trends are, to a large extent, centred around the versatile range of modern day mini-trucks. In fact, customizing these economical runabouts has developed into practically a national pastime in the United States. Numerous firms are specialising in conversion kits and accessories to suit every type of mini-trucker.

For instance, the muscular-looking 'stepside' conversion is a firm favourite with the street crowd. It consists of a substitute narrow cargo bed positioned between bulbous rear fenders, which, combined with a slightly chopped roof gives a tough gutsy look. Add to this; an integrated chin spoiler and fender flares, a neatly designed tube grille, rectangular headlights, mag wheels, graphic or single tone paint scheme and a fully upholstered cab, and you'll have the archetypal California street truck. Obviously, you could incorporate many of these ideas within a sedan conversion for a real 'trick truck' effect.

Detachable camper tops have become very popular, widening the appeal of the pick-ups as a dual purpose work and leisure machine. Although they are available 'off the shelf' for most modern trucks, a custom-made structure will often separate a classy camper from the rest.

Further to the outdoor leisure theme, the latest vehicle craze to sweep America is the high and mighty off-road pick-up. More and more people are looking away from the street for their automotive fun, and these four-wheel drive monsters provide a comfortable way of reaching otherwise inaccessible areas. The typical dealer's lot 'boonie-basher' is a late model pick-up, incorporating 'spoker' wheels and dirt tyres, graphic paint scheme, extra lights, roll bar and heavy-duty suspension. Equipped with every fashionable extra, new four-by's are very expensive. However, with enough ingenuity and parts swapping, it's possible to convert many older vehicles to serve exactly the same purpose, at a fraction of the cost.

Top left: Slick rig reflects detailed under hood treatment and neat bodywork. *Top right:* Stepside looks tough from behind. *Above:* Custom campers can look good. *Centre right:* This chopped fleetside sits low and mean. *Left:* A sanitary clean 1949 Chevy. *Right:* It seems unlikely that this chromium-plated 4WD monster has ever seen off-road dirt.

Making Good

Project custom cars, particularly the older type, invariably begin their new lives in a sad state of repair. It may be that your potential dream machine is sitting on the lower deck of the local wrecker's yard. Body panels missing, doors and fenders riddled with rust — the sort of challenge that such a vehicle represents is possibly the underlying reason for starting a custom venture. On the other hand, it may be the only surviving example of a rare model that falls within your price range. Either way, a lot of hard work will be necessary to get the body back into shape. Whatever restoration task you decide to take on, approach it with a methodical attitude and be patient. The end result will be worth it.

Removing dents

Apart from slight surface depressions that can be safely filled with plastic filler, dents usually come in three variations — those that can be reached from both sides and generally beaten out, others that appear in double skinned panels and can only be reached from the front, and deeply creased areas that are usually beyond satisfactory repair.

Your first move is to go round the entire car feeling for dents. Take your time and inspect each panel separately, circling the affected areas with a piece of chalk or a felt tip pen.

The next thing to establish is whether the dent in question can be successfully straightened out. A prime example of damage that cannot be easily restored is where a front or rear fender has suffered accident damage and the metal is severely stretched and distorted. In these sorts of cases you will need to replace the complete panel or, if this is not possible, cut out the damaged section and weld in new metal.

The idea behind rectifying any repairable dent is to beat or pull it out as near to the original body contour as possible, before filling and sanding to a smooth finish. To do this successfully you will need to use the right tools.

The most useful tool is the panel beater's planishing hammer. It has smooth polished faces, one being square and perfectly flat, the other round and slightly domed. Its main use is for the smoothing and finalizing of the beating process and it is used in conjunction with a solid lump of steel called a dolly block. There are a wide range of dolly blocks available, all moulded to common panel or fender contours. Unless you are faced with a number of varying contours, a general purpose dolly should be sufficient for most areas.

A useful tool for 'picking up' low areas on the surface of a panel is the pick hammer. As well as having a pointed 'pick' end this hammer also incorporates a round face.

Another handy tool for locating low spots and smoothing the 'planished' surface is the adjustable body file. It can be adapted to file the surface of almost any shaped panel.

A professional body repair man will carry an extensive range of tools so that he can achieve a near perfect finish and lessen the need for any final body filler. However, this standard of finish requires both skill and dexterity so you must be prepared to use more filler than an expert would require.

Panel beating techniques

Where a dent is accessible from both sides, your first job is to clean off any road dirt and undersealant from the underside, using a scraper and a wire brush. If such materials are not removed a pimpled surface will result as the panel is re-shaped.

If you are tackling a deep dent, the next stage involves working the dent back roughly to shape. In most cases this can be achieved by using the dolly block on its own. The dolly should be of a similar shape to that of the original contour of the damaged section. Ideally, you are aiming to hit the centre of the dent with the dolly with a force equal and opposite to that which caused the damage in the first place (1). However, it is advisable to do this process in a series of follow through actions rather than strike an almighty blow and stretch the panel out too far (1a, 1b). This action will necessitate shrinking the metal, which normally involves the use of a high temperature gas welding flame. If you are handling a flimsy section of metal, e.g. the edge of a fender, use your other hand to improve the rigidity of the panel and so increase the effectiveness of each blow.

When the dent is roughly to shape, or if the damage is not so serious, you can use the hammer and dolly combination to smooth out the surface further.

A technique known as 'indirect hammering' can be used where an outward/high area stands adjacent to an inward/low area. Hold the dolly beneath the low area (2) then, using the square end of the hammer to distribute an even force, direct light blows at the peak of the adjacent ridge. As a result of receiving the hammer blow indirectly, the dolly will be forced away from the dent (2a). But, if you apply enough pressure to the dolly, it will return to impart a second blow to the area. As you increase this pressure, the dent will gradually flatten out (2b). However, don't beat the panel out too far and stretch the metal. It's much safer to leave a slight dent that can be filled later on. Any minor high spots can

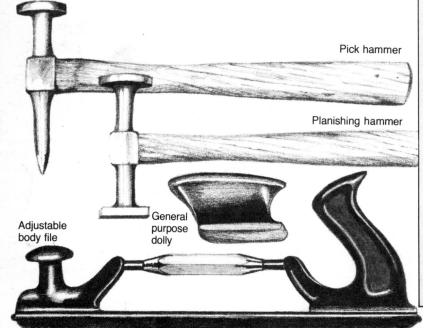

Pick hammer

Planishing hammer

Adjustable body file

General purpose dolly

usually be flattened by incorporating a 'direct hammering' technique. Hold the dolly directly under the high spot and commence with light hammer blows (3). If the high area takes the form of a long ridge, work progressively from end to end until the metal is seated on the face of the dolly. Having eliminated the high spots there may still be some low spots in evidence. Now you can use the pick hammer. Make a few light taps in the centre of the low area using the 'pick' end of the hammer (4). This should stretch the surrounding metal just enough to raise the surface (4a). You can then revert back to the hammer and dolly to tap down the points made by the end of the pick.

When the surface of the panel feels almost smooth, use the adjust-able body file to remove any scores or scratches and to reveal any minor low areas still present. Adjust the blade so that it does not quite match up with the contour to be filed, leaving about ⅛ inch (3mm) clearance at each end. Hold the file in both hands and apply long, light, forward strokes, parallel to each other over the whole area. Don't draw the file back over the surface as this tends to dull the cutting edge of the blade. If you are filing a large area, change the direction of the stroke as the work progresses, for the smoothest possible finish. Always bear in mind that the strength of the panel is dependent on its thickness, so never remove too much metal from the surface. After filing, the surface will be ready for final levelling with plastic filler.

Dents in double skinned panels

Dents that occur in double skinned panels, such as doors, must be liter-ally pulled out using a different method. Drill a hole in the centre of the dent and fix in a self-tapping screw. Hold the screw head with a pair of mole grips or pliers and pull it out gently. If you are tackling a long indentation, use several screws at regular intervals and pull on each one consecutively. Again, do not pull too hard or you will be left with proud areas. Any minor high spots can usually be tapped back with the planishing hammer. Obviously, where there is no access to the underside of the dent, you will rely more on the use of plastic filler to gain a perfect finish.

The success you are able to achieve with panel beating techni-ques depends entirely on the intui-tive control you have over the tools. Therefore, it is advisable to buy an old fender or door panel from the local wrecker's yard, make a number of dents in it, and practice their correction before you attempt any repair work on your own car.

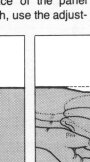

1 *Hold dolly beneath centre of low area.*

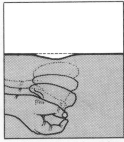

1a *Hit low area in series of follow through actions.*

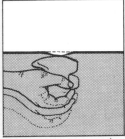

1b *The dent will gradually flatten out.*

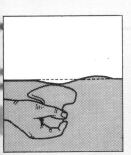

2 *Hold dolly beneath low area.*

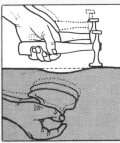

2a *Direct light blows at peak of adjacent ridge.*

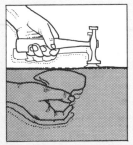

2b *While applying pres-sure to dolly from behind.*

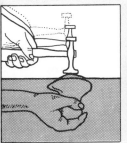

3 *Hold dolly under high spot and commence with light blows.*

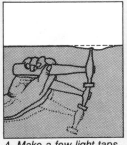

4 *Make a few light taps in centre of low area.*

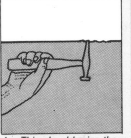

4a *This should raise the surface just enough...*

Repairing rust damage

You may be fortunate in owning a vehicle that has been well cared for and is virtually rust free, but as is normally the case, your project custom car will probably be showing various signs of corrosion.

Rust is the biggest enemy in any steel bodied auto. It occurs when water or condensation settles on bare metal and sets up an electro-chemical reaction. The worst cases always start from the inside edge of a panel, where mud and water gets trapped and the metal is starved of air. As the rust spreads from the inside out, blisters and holes appear in the surface. If the holes are only minor they can usually be patched with glass fibre, or perforated metal and filler. However, extensive rust damage will usually necessitate welding in new metal or, better still, a replacement panel.

Surface rust

The first thing to do is locate all the affected areas. Inspect each panel with a critical eye, as the smallest of blemishes will lead to further deterioration if neglected.

The process for repairing slight surface rust, usually caused by stone chips or scratches, is quite straightforward. You will need a few sheets of 40 and 80 grit abrasive paper, some 180 dry paper, and a rubber block (available from auto paint suppliers). Cut a piece of 40 grit paper into four equal parts and wrap one piece around the flat edge of the rubber block. You can then physically rub the affected area, removing the paint and all traces of rust until all that remains is shiny bare metal (1). Whilst sanding the area you must attempt to 'feather' the paint edges (2). Feathering is a term given to blending the edges of a repair smoothly from bare metal, through primer to the surrounding paintwork. After the initial surface has been cut back, change to 80 grit, then 180 dry paper for feathering. Wherever possible, always use the rubber block when sanding and never use the tips of your fingers as this will leave 'tram lines' or ridges in the surface.

If there are a number of blemishes in any one area, it is wiser to sand the entire section to bare metal, rather than have a mass of feathered edges. In such cases, an electric drill used with a coarse sanding disc, say 120 grit, or a professional orbital air sander wi[ll] make the work a lot easier.

Whenever the original paintwork is removed the bare metal should be treated with an anti-rust preparation as soon as possible (3). It only take[s] a few minutes for oxidation to start especially if the weather is damp. Some makes of rust inhibitor mus[t] be washed off after application and neutralized with methylated spirits so always follow the manufacturers instructions.

Holes and blistered paint

Areas where rust has eaten righ[t] through the metal or where the oute[r] surface shows signs of blistering should be sanded 8 – 10 inches (20–25cms) beyond the immediate visible damage (4). If you use a high-speed electric sander, it's advisable to wear shatterproo[f] goggles as bits of metal will often break away and fly off.

After sanding off all the paint you will be left with either a rust hole or a corroded honeycomb effect. Cu[t] away any remaining rust with a pai[r] of snips or sheet metal cutters, the[n] file back the edges until you reach good sound metal (5 and 6). Clean the underside with a stiff wire brush to remove any debris, then sand back a couple of inches (5cms) o[f] bright metal around the hole. If the damage occurs on double skinned panels, where access to the underside is limited, use a piece of bent metal to scrape off any dirt and pou[r] small amounts of white spirit around the edges of the hole.

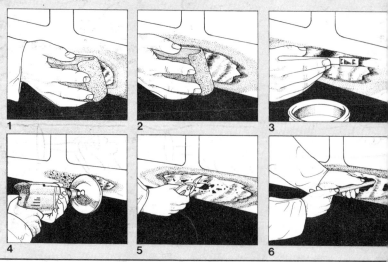

1 2 3

4 5 6

Using glass fibre

If the holes appear in non-structural areas and are accessible from both sides, they can be bridged with glass fibre, which is available in various thicknesses and textures. It is very pliable and when impregnated with a resin/hardener mixture, sets to form a tough skin. You will need to use chopped strand matt for large holes that require strong reinforcement. Smaller holes can generally be patched with glass fibre fabric.

Cut out two or three pieces of glass fibre so they extend about 2 inches (5cms) beyond the edge of the hole (1). Mix up the resin and hardener according to the directions in the container and lay one piece on a clean non-stick surface, such as polythene. You can then impregnate the matt with the resin mixture using a short, stiff bristled brush (2). Apply the mixture to the bare metal at the back of the hole then place the glass fibre behind the damage, holding it in place until it cures (3). Always remember to put polythene over your hand or, alternatively, support the glass fibre with a piece of waxed card. Now apply more resin hardener mixture to the back of the glass fibre, then impregnate the next piece and place it in position as before. You can repeat this process until the desired strength is achieved. What was once a hole is now a surface dent that can be levelled smooth with plastic filler.

Using perforated metal

Holes in double skinned panels are approached in a different way, using perforated zinc or aluminium. Cut a piece of perforated metal so that it is slightly bigger than the hole but can be passed through it at an angle (4). This will be easy with an irregular-shaped hole, but if it is almost circular, you may have to fold the metal slightly. Push a long screw into one of the central perforations and turn it until it is tight. Mix an adequate amount of filler using a fairly high proportion of hardener so that it cures quickly. Apply this to the bare metal at the back of the hole and to the edge of the perforated metal on the screw head side. Using the screw to manoeuvre the patch, pass it through the hole and pull it back so that it is held in contact with the underside (5). Hold it in place until the filler hardens then remove the screw. You can then apply more filler from the front to complete the repair.

Where an edge section has disintegrated, cut a piece of perforated metal to match the missing area, allowing the appropriate distance for the underside overlap. Also allow enough extra width along the side of the metal which will be used to form the new edge section, e.g. about ½ inch (1.25cms) for the edge of a door. You can then fold this extra width back to form a radiused edge, smaller than that of the existing edge, to allow for filler build-up (6).

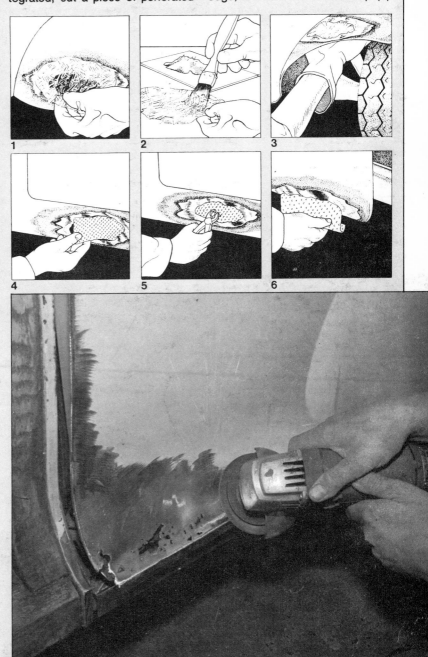

Using plastic filler

Plastic body filler is one of the most useful materials to any customizer. It can be moulded to almost any required shape and relied upon to give a good hard finish that will not shrink or crack with age. It is most commonly used to fill minor body dents, or holes that have been previously bridged. With a bit of time and patience you can achieve a finish that will be indistinguishable from the original body contour.

Surface preparation

Before you think about applying any filler the surface must be properly prepared. Sand an area to bare metal larger than that to be filled and feather it with the surrounding paintwork. This will allow you to spread the filler beyond the actual damage and ensure a smooth, balanced build-up. Filler will not bond properly to paint and this mistake is often responsible for imperfections in the final paint finish.

To ensure good adhesion between filler and metal, scribe a criss-cross pattern into the heart of the dent or low spot, using the end of a file or screwdriver (1). Take care not to scratch the surrounding metal.

To minimise the chances of any future rusting, treat the area with an anti-rust preparation. This precaution is advisable even though many fillers contain an anti-rust agent.

Mixing

Most makes of filler come in two parts, a resin base and a hardener or catalyst. The catalyst is usually a different colour so you can establish a good mix when the filler becomes a uniform tone. Your best choice of mixing board is a piece of thin plastic about 6 inches (15cms) square. As well as being free of any foreign matter that may contaminate the paste, it can be cleaned of hardened filler by flexing.

Always follow the manufacturers' instructions when mixing and mix only enough for the job in hand. If you prepare too much at once it will harden and become unusable before it can be applied. Add the hardener to the resin by laying it in with a flat knife (2).

Application

Apply the filler over the area using a plastic spreader which will be supplied with the kit. Use a sideways downwards motion and push it firmly into the dent extending a few inches/centimetres beyond the damaged area (3). You can then skim the filler surface until it is slightly proud of the bare metal, using a 12 inch (30cms) steel rule on the larger areas.

If the area to be filled is more than ¼ inch (6mm) deep, build up the surface with thin layers of filler for maximum strength, allowing each one to dry before applying the next. This will take about 30 minutes under normal weather conditions. Don't be too impatient and add a lot of hardener as it will weaken the end result.

Shaping

After the filler has set, but before it has fully hardened, it will be ready for shaping. Use a cheese grater file and a very light touch to cut the filler back roughly to shape, but still slightly proud of the surrounding metal (4). Let it harden for a while longer, then continue shaping and smoothing with 80 grit productic paper. A hand size rubber block w aid an even finish when sandir small repairs, but if you are dealir with larger flatter areas, wrap th paper around a long flat block f best results. Make frequent check for any contour errors by runnin clean water over the surface whil looking along it. If you see any lo spots, clean and dry the whole are and spread in some more filler.

Finishing

As the repair nears the corre shape, switch to successively fin grades of abrasive paper. Finis with 220 grit used with plenty soapy water, until the textures of th filler and the surrounding paintwor match and feather perfectly (5).

If after cleaning the area wit fresh water you find any pin hole: chips or low spots, the best way dealing with them is to use putty Apply a thin layer of putty, firmly bu smoothly over the imperfection using a plastic spreader, and leave to dry thoroughly. You can then we sand the puttied areas with a fin grade of paper, say 400 grit, the spray two coats of primer/surface over the entire repair area (6). Afte sanding it's worth making a las check for any surface irregularitie that may otherwise be accentuate by the final paint coats.

1 Scribe a criss-cross pattern into heart of area.

2 Lay hardener into resin with flat knife.

3 Spread filler a few inches (centimetres) beyond damaged area.

4 Cut the filler back roughly to shape.

5 Sand until perfectly smooth.

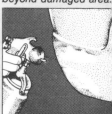
6 Spray primer/surface over the entire area.

Welding

The previously mentioned methods of repair are adequate within low stress areas such as doors or fenders. However, never use fibreglass, perforated metal or filler within high stress areas such as chassis members or pressed steel panels that support suspension units. In these areas damaged sections are replaced by welding in new metal which contains similar characteristics to the original.

In welding, two pieces of metal are held together and heated until the edges melt and fuse. Additional molten metal is then added to increase the strength of the weld.

If you intend doing any serious body modifications or rebuilding an early car, a practical knowledge of welding equipment, techniques and applications is essential. It will enable you to pursue ambitious ideas such as roof chopping or chassis building. It's a good idea to enrol at an evening class at a local college where you will receive firsthand practical training. Never attempt any welding job unless you are fully aware of the potential dangers involved.

Gas welding

The most versatile method of welding is known as gas welding, whereby two gases — oxygen and acetylene — are mixed together and ignited to produce an extremely high temperature flame. This flame, emitted from the tip of a hand held welding torch, is directed at the join of the two metals until they melt. Extra molten metal from a filler rod is added to the seam which, on cooling, becomes as strong as the base metal.

Gas or 'oxyacetylene' fusion welding is commonly used in sheet metal bodywork, utilizing a steel filler rod. This requires skill to avoid metal distortion caused by the high temperatures involved. Consequently, some bodymen prefer to 'braze' panel steel, a non-fusion method which requires less heat. Gas welding can be used for a variety of different applications and metal thicknesses.

Equipment

You will need oxygen and acetylene gas in cylinders, regulators and pressure gauges, hoses, a welding torch, a supply of filler rods, goggles, gloves, a welding manual and a spark lighter.

For safety reasons, the gas cylinders should always be handled very carefully and kept upright at all times. They should never be used or stored in or near hot temperatures as this may cause a fatal explosion. Also, oil and grease are incompatible with these gases, so never oil or grease any part of the equipment.

The purpose of both the oxygen and acetylene regulators is to provide a continuous flow of gas at the required pressure. Most regulators are equipped with gauges which indicate the amount of pressure in the cylinders, and the working pressure in the hoses and torch.

Different coloured hoses carry the gases to the torch — blue or green for oxygen, red for acetylene.

The welding torch serves to mix the gases, and has a handle for directing the flame. An 'equal pressure' torch is widely used in automotive work, operating with the same pressure for both gases. A copper welding tip is installed at the end of the torch to provide a safe method of varying the amount of heat to the weld. They come in various sizes, depending on the thickness of metal you are welding — consult the manufacturers' manual for the correct size to use. The job in hand will also determine what sort of filler rod(s) you will need. Generally, they should have the same composition and be of equal thickness to the 'parent' metal. Always wear colour-tinted goggles and asbestos gloves for personal safety whilst welding.

Equipment assembly

There is a proper sequence in setting up gas welding equipment which you should always follow for maximum safety. First, check that the cylinders are secured within their carrying trolley. Remove the cylinder valve caps and wipe the valve threads with a clean dry cloth. Open the valves slightly, then close them again quickly. This process is referred to as 'cracking' open the cylinders, and the purpose of it is to blow out any dirt or obstructions that may be present in the valves. Crack open each cylinder in turn.

Now attach each regulator to its appropriate cylinder valve, using a proper wrench designed for this purpose. The oxygen regulator will have a right handed thread, the acetylene left. Connect the oxygen hose, which also has a right hand thread connector to the oxygen regulator. Open the regulator to 5 p.s.i. to blow out any dust from the hose, and close it again quickly. Now connect the acetylene hose connector to the acetylene regulator and blow out any dust in the same manner. Make sure there are no naked flames or oily/greasy rags within the vicinity, which could cause an explosion.

Attach the torch or 'blow pipe' to the other end of the hoses, noting that while the hose connections may be a different size at the torch than at the regulators, they still have right and left hand threads. The oxygen connection will be marked 'OXY' or 'OXYGEN', the acetylene 'ACY' or 'FUEL'. Finally, check that the control valves on the blow pipe are closed and install the appropriate size of welding tip into the blow pipe.

The flame

The actual 'tool' of gas welding is the flame, which must be of the proper size and shape. By adjusting the proportions of oxygen and acetylene you can produce three different types of flame — neutral, carburizing and oxidizing.

A neutral flame, with a sharply defined cone, results when the two gases are mixed in equal proportions and is used in the majority of welding jobs.

If more oxygen is present than acetylene, the resultant flame is said to be oxidizing, whereas an excess of acetylene will produce a carburizing flame. These are used when welding brass and for building up worn surfaces, respectively.

To obtain a neutral flame, partially open the oxygen valve on the torch and adjust the oxygen regulator until the pressure rises to the required amount (dependent on the tip size). Now close the valve. Repeat the operation to obtain the acetylene gas supply. Now open the torch acetylene valve just under half a turn and, with the tip pointing away from you or anything inflammable, light the gas with a spark lighter held at right angles to the tip. Continue opening the valve until the excess smoke disappears and the flame leaves the end of the torch by about ⅛ inch (3mm). You can then close the valve slightly so that the flame returns to the tip. Open the oxygen valve on the torch until the feathered edges of the flame disappear into the end of the sharp inner cone. You now have a neutral flame.

Preparation of metals

The metals must be properly prepared by cutting out all traces of rust, cleaning both edges to shiny bare metal, and de-greasing. Paint will prevent the metal from heating up and will also contaminate the weld.

Make a cardboard template of the area you are replacing, adding, or otherwise modifying, and cut a piece of metal accordingly. In body repair work, the metal should be of equal thickness and match the profile of the existing panel. An alternative to hand-forming difficult shapes or contours is to find an identical panel which is in good shape and cut out the required section from it.

The usual type of weld employed in sheet metal work is the butt weld, where the two edges to be united are abutted together. Clamp the pieces in position with C clamps or similar, so that there is no more than a 1/16 inch (1.5mm) gap at any part. You can then make small temporary tack welds at each end, then every 2 or 3 inches (5 or 7.5cms) along the seam. This 'distortion precaution' will help to maintain proper alignment when the finish weld is being made.

Gas welding techniques

There are two methods you can use in oxyacetylene welding — 'leftward' or 'rightward' welding. Leftward welding is the accepted method of joining unbevelled material under ⅛ inch (3mm) thickness. The rightward method is more difficult, recommended for steel plate over 3/16 inch (4.5mm) thick. The following text deals with leftward welding, the method employed in light gauge panel work.

Grip the torch in one hand so that you have complete control over it, while holding the filler rod in the other. Maintain the inner cone of the neutral flame approximately ⅛ inch (3mm) above the work, and pointed in the direction in which the weld is to proceed. If you are right handed, this will be from right to left. The flame should make an angle of about 60 degrees with the work for efficient heat penetration. Hold the flame in one spot until the metals start to melt. As soon as a molten pool is formed, place the filler rod in it so that the angle between the rod and the flame is 90 degrees. Now proceed along the seam, moving the flame in a small circular fashion whilst adding extra metal to the weld as necessary. Regular timing of the hand movements will produce an even wave form to the completed weld. In most cases it's advisable to finish weld a seam in alternate sections between the initial tack welds, as a further safeguard against metal distortion.

If you are dealing with an uphill situation, work from the bottom and proceed vertically. In sheet metal work the flame should make an angle of about 30 degrees with the vertical surface, the filler rod 90 degrees to the flame.

When the completed weld has cooled down, lightly grind the ridge with a flexible disc sander and check for any high or low spots. These can be flattened with a hammer and dolly and skimmed with plastic filler where necessary.

Hammer welding

This technique is often used in custom bodywork, where a combination of maximum strength and metal control/minimum filler is needed, e.g. a top chop. It involves an alternate use of the torch and the planishing hammer/dolly, i.e. welding a short 2 inch (5cm) section between light tack welds, using the hammer/dolly to flatten the ridge or 'bead', welding another section, and so on. This technique can only be used where there is access to the underside of the panel. It also requires perfect mating of the two edges prior to welding, for minimum use of filler rod and the smallest possible bead. The torch tip should be held flatter to the plane of travel than normal, and the filler rod held at an opposite low angle. You'll need a stand on which to put the lighted torch when hammering.

Brazing

Another metal joining method that utilizes gas welding equipment is brazing. It is particularly applicable to sheet metal work, as the relatively low temperatures involved minimize the possibilities of panel distortion.

There are two types of brazing. The first is actually called brazing, where a closely fitted joint is filled by capillary action of the molten filler material, a non-ferrous metal or alloy with a lower melting point than that of the metals being joined. The second, known as braze-welding, does not depend on capillary action. The base metals are not melted, but the non-ferrous filler rod fills an open groove joint and makes a definite bead, as in a conventional gas fusion weld. Although not actually fusing the metals together, brazing does effectively join or bond them.

By selecting the right grade of filler rod, brazing can be used on steels, copper, brasses, stainless steels and many other alloys. It makes possible the joining of two dissimilar metals, such as brass to steel or steel to copper, and is also useful for repairing parts that have to be re-chromed.

Brazing panel steel

The basic technique for brazing panel steel is similar to that of welding, but instead of a mild steel filler rod, you use a flux-coated, copper-base rod. Flux is a chemical powder that dissolves oxides, prevents oxidation and cleans the metal being worked on. Filler rods are available in pre-fluxed form or those that must be heated and dipped into a tin of powdered flux prior to the actual brazing operation. Although they are more expensive to buy, pre-fluxed ods are easier to work with.

Brazing requires perfect metal preparation and, for utmost strength, the surfaces should be positioned almost flush. Flames and pressures are kept the same for similar thickness materials as gas welding, that is, neutral for panel steel.

Hold the torch at the same angle as for leftward welding and with the tip of the cone about ⅛ inch (3mm) above the metal; warm it to a dull red. Now touch the metal with the fluxed rod and tack the joint. The molten filler material will be drawn between the two pieces (capillary action). Tack every couple of inches (five centimetres), or whatever distance seems necessary. Having completed the tack spots, go back to your starting point and, playing the flame in a circular motion along its path, braze the whole joint.

If, for example, you were 'braze-welding' a closed corner fillet joint (where the two metals are at right angles) you would tack as before, form a pool of molten filler material and feed the rod into it, building up the desired thickness along the joint.

After the finished joint has cooled down slightly, wash off the shiny glass-like coating of flux with warm water. On a braze-weld, it may be necessary to chip away any stubborn bits with a hammer. Don't overlook this job otherwise your final paint job will flake away as the flux decomposes. All that remains is to grind and fill where necessary.

Shutting down procedure

When you have finished welding or brazing, close the acetylene control valve on the torch, then the oxygen valve. Shut off the cylinder supply valves, then open and close the torch valves (oxygen first, then acetylene) to relieve pressure in the system. Make certain that the gauges register zero. Finally, wind back both regulator adjusting screws.

Arc welding

If you intend building a ground-up street rod, that is constructing your own chassis, engine mounts, bracketry etc., you'll need to know how to handle an arc welder. Generally speaking, electric arc welding is best suited to medium or heavy gauge material because of the extremely high temperatures involved. However, with enough practical experience and a unit that incorporates infinitely variable controls, it is possible to arc-weld thin sheet metal, though definitely not an exercise for the beginner.

The process relies on the fact that if a heavy electrical current passes across a very small gap between an electrode and the metal workpiece, an arc is struck and a great deal of heat is generated. The arc, which is in effect a continuous spark, melts the metals, forming a molten puddle. Extra metal needed to substantiate the weld is added as the flux-coated electrode melts into the puddle. As the arc is moved the molten metal solidifies and fusion takes place.

Equipment and safety

There are many portable arc welding plants on the market that operate off a household mains electric supply. Your choice of unit will be governed by the range or thickness of materials you intend welding, and the necessary amperage output needed to perform the work. In building a street rod, a welder with 225 amps maximum output will be more than sufficient for welding bracketry etc. up to ½ inch (1.25cms) thick. A cheaper 30/130 amp unit will be good for ¼ inch (6mm) metal. These DIY units usually include all the accessories you need — a selection of electrode rods, a flux chipping hammer, clamps and cables, and a safety-approved face mask; most important as the arc will seriously damage the naked eye.

Always remember that you will be handling live electricity and if you somehow manage to make your body part of the circuit you'll receive a very nasty shock. Electricity flows from the welding machine through a cable to the welding tool, down the electrode and across the arc to the workpiece. It then returns to the machine via an earth clamp and return lead which is affixed to the metal, so never touch the workpiece or clamp when welding and allow plenty of time for it to cool down.

Preparation

As with other metal joining methods, the surface should be free of rust and clean, both at the point of welding and at the earth clamp, to ensure a good flow of current. Prior to tack welding, the metals are clamped in position as before or, in the case of a chassis build-up, jigged into place. On butt joints, the plates should be 1/24 to 1/12 inch (1 to 2mm) apart with abutting edges bevelled if the plates are over ¼ inch (6mm) thick, although you'll probably perform far more fillet welds with arc welding equipment. Choose an electrode suitable for the gauge of material you are welding and set the amperage control to the level recommended on a chart which should be supplied with the kit.

Striking the arc and manipulation

You should be relaxed in a comfortable position so that you can weld across from right to left rather than towards or away from yourself. Hold the rod at an angle of about 60 degrees to the surface and 1 inch (2.5cms) above it. Place the mask in front of your eyes, then touch the surface of the metal with the tip of the electrode, using a movement similar to that of striking a match. Once the arc has been struck the electrode will melt, and a downward movement of the electrode holder will be required to maintain the arc at the correct length (⅛ inch (3mm) from the molten pool). The tip must also be moved along at a sufficient rate to avoid too large a build-up of molten metal in one place. If you watch the arc closely at all times the combined movement will come naturally. At the end of a run, pull the rod away from the surface quickly to avoid splatter.

After enough practise you should be able to form a nice even bead, where the slag settles in an easily removed layer on top of the weld. When chipping off slag, always keep the mask in front of your eyes or wear proper goggles.

If a joint is going to be very deep, where one run is not enough, the weld should be built up in successive layers, chipping away all slag between each run.

Customizing Ideas

As previously mentioned, good planning is the most important aspect of a successful project — establishing a theme and incorporating the right modifications/improvements that will heighten the overall effect, within a logical build-up process.

Before you make any exterior changes, trace over several enlarged photographs of your car in its basic shape and pencil in all your ideas, whether mild or radical. You will then be able to see if they work individually and, more important, as a whole.

Glassfibre techniques

Glass fibre, or glass reinforced plastic, is a very useful material for constructing non-stressed auto body parts. It is light, non-corrosive, inexpensive and quite strong enough for normal applications. Most important of all, it's easy to work with using the minimum of special tools or equipment. With a basic knowledge of glass fibre laminating and mould construction, you can design and make your own fender flares, spoilers, replacement panels and so on.

The material used in GRP construction is actually a hard setting polyester resin into which any of several types of glass fibre reinforcements are embedded. The method of moulding is described as 'laying up' which refers to the fact that one or more layers of matting or fabric are manually laid on or in the mould after application of the wet resin. Different resins are used for the initial or 'gel' coat (a tough surface skin), and for subsequent coats in combination with the fibres, although each has to be mixed with a catalyst to induce it to harden. Prior to application of the resin mixture, the mould is coated with a releasing agent to enable the finished product to be easily removed when cured.

In most cases the actual mould is laid up from glass fibre. If you are copying an existing shape that has a smooth outer surface, e.g. a fender, you can use this as a male mould on which to construct a female mould, in which to make the finished product. To make something from scratch with a smooth outer surface, you'll first have to build a male pattern or 'plug' on which to lay up your female mould, again in which to make your finished item. If you require a smooth inner surface (e.g. where an object such as an air duct will be recessed and bonded beneath a panel opening) you can mould the finished item directly from

the plug. Since the quality of the end product is directly dependent on the finish of the plug, choose fine-grain material(s) that can be easily shaped and sanded. The most commonly used are wood, hardboard, metal, polyurethane foam and plastic body filler.

Most of the leading glass fibre manufacturers market D.I.Y. kits which contain all the tools and materials you are likely to need for the laminating process. They usually include a brush to apply the resin, a special metal roller for removing air bubbles when the glass is laid up, and a few pairs of protective gloves. Always follow the maker's instructions on mixing ratios, handling of materials etc.

Your working environment should be clean and well ventilated — inhaling concentrated resin fumes can be very dangerous. It also needs to be quite warm, ideally 18–20°C. In cold conditions resins take a long time to harden, and gel coats will be difficult to apply. Never smoke within the working area as most of the materials are highly inflammable.

Before you attempt anything too ambitious it's advisable to have a practise run in order to get the feel of the process. Try something simple, such as a slab-sided hood scoop, or a rectangular/square box-shape, that could be used as a recess for a license plate.

The laminating process
A simple license plate recess can be made in one process — direct from the plug, since it is the smooth inside surface that will be exposed

Start by taking the exact measurements of the plate, or its chrome surround. Decide what depth of recess you require (normally about 2 inches (5cms) on flat panels and select a piece of wood of equal thickness, and appropriate size. You can then transfer the measurements, allowing an extra ¼ inch (6mm) all round, and cut the wood accordingly. Concentrate on getting all the sides exactly square and perfectly smooth. If you require radiused inner edges, carefully shape the edges of the wood likewise. A small flange, or lip, will enable easy bonding to the back of the panel. This can be incorporated into the moulding by fixing a piece of hardboard (1 inch (25mm) oversize) to the base of the wood, filling any slight gaps with plastic wood filler. The following process (plug/mould preparation and 'laying up') can be applied to almost any object you may wish to make.

When you have a perfectly finished plug, it needs to be coated with a polyester surfacer and lightly sanded (1). As well as sealing the wood, it will hold the subsequent layers of release wax. These are applied with a clean cloth and polished between each coat (2). Always follow the manufacturers instructions as to the number of coats. To complete the preparation stage, spray or sponge on a very thin coat of polyvinyl alcohol or PVA. This is impervious to resin and ensures no sticking occurs.

Next comes the actual production of the finished item, starting with the gel coat. The resin used for this purpose is quite thick in consistency. Mix the catalyst hardener into a suitable quantity of resin, 2–4% measured by weight with a syringe is recommended (3). Always wear protective gloves, and keep them well away from your eyes. Brush the mix onto the plug and try to get an even coverage which is neither too thick or too thin, particularly in the corners (4). Allow the gel coat to dry to a tacky finish. This will take about 45 minutes under normal conditions. While you are waiting, cut the glass fibre matt to the approximate size and shape, allowing at least 1 inch (25mm) overhang which can be trimmed off later.

Matts and fabrics are available in a wide range of densities or weights, although ordinary 1oz. (300g) is always best applied first behind the gel coat. It consists of random strewn strands of glass filaments, bound together with a substance that dissolves in the lay up resin. Two layers of 1oz. (300g) matt is

removed. A metal roller will help this process (6). Pay particular attention to sharp edges or corners as it is important that the matt solidly reinforces the gel coat in these areas. When you are satisfied that all air pockets have been expelled, lay up your next piece of matt and repeat the process.

The moulding will be partly set within about half an hour, and this is the best time to trim off the excess matt. Use a sharp razor knife and take care not to distort the finished product (7).

Separating the moulding from the plug is likely to be easier the longer you leave it in place. A full cure

reaching maximum hardness and strength takes at least a week. It may need a bit of 'gentle persuasion', in which case use a thin piece of wood and carefully prize round the edges (8). If there is pronounced sticking you can introduce warm water which should dissolve the PVA and aid separation. When the moulding is free, wash it thoroughly in warm water and detergent to remove all traces of release wax.

If the article is to be a female mould for a finished product, coat and polish the smooth surface with wax and PVA release, and repeat the laying up process as before.

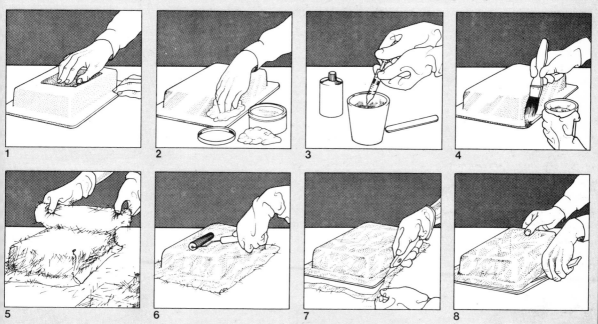

usually adequate for most finished mouldings. However, if you are constructing an intermediate female mould from the plug, it needs to be at least twice as thick, say two layers of 2oz. (600g) matt over the initial 1oz. (300g) layer. Fabrics are normally used where a combination of high strength and flexibility is required, e.g. deck lid, doors etc.

When the gel coat has cured sufficiently, brush on a liberal coat of catalysed lay up resin, then place (lay up) the matt on top of the plug (5). You can then stipple in more resin until no dry fibres remain and all the air bubbles have been

Frenching

Frenching, or tunnelling, is one of the oldest and most effective custom body tricks. As the latter term infers, it is the art of recessing exterior obtrusions in order to create clean, simple lines..

The basic process is quite straightforward and can be applied in several imaginative ways to aerials (electrically operated look most impressive), tail-lights, license plates and so on. Recesses can be round, oval, square, or any shape you like, depending on the object(s) in question. For example, you may wish to replace your stock tail-lights with separate sidelight/indicator units from another vehicle. The new items could either be frenched individually as normal, or side by side within a complementary shape. That is, a shape that harmonizes with the area of the car you are dealing with, as well as neatly enclosing the objects themselves.

A popular technique is to mount the actual tunnel slightly proud of the surrounding bodywork, and gently radius the edge with plastic filler. If well executed, this can add a lot of style.

Tunnelling an aerial

A radio aerial is often the mos[t] necessary, yet visually undesirable accessory for your custom, so wh[y] not do the obvious thing and bury [it] within a panel?

Firstly, you'll need a length [of] steel tubing of the correct diamete[r] so that the base assembly fit[s] snugly within it. To ensure that th[e] aerial stands vertical and centra[l] when tunnelled, cut one end o[f] perfectly square. Find an old washe[r] of equal diameter to serve as [a] blanking piece, and enlarge the hol[e] to accommodate the aerial (1). Yo[u] can then weld the washer to th[e] square end of the tube. Before yo[u] go any further, drill an 1/8 inch (3mm[)] drain hole near the base, otherwis[e] the tunnel will fill up with rain-wate[r.]

If you are inserting the aeri[al] within a flat panel, cover the are[a] with masking tape, and draw roun[d] the open end of the tube to mark th[e] exact position of the body hole (2[).] With deeply crowned or slopin[g] panels, make up a cardboard tem[-] plate and transfer the eliptical shap[e] onto the body.

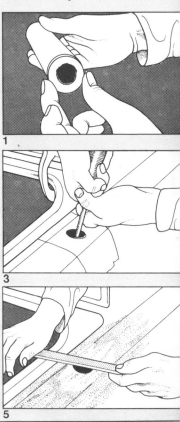

Drill a hole dead centre and file it out carefully so that the tube fits as tight as possible (3). Remove the tube and cut it down to about 3 inches (7.5cms) total length. Now grind or sand away all traces of paint from the edges of the hole in preparation for the final fixing.

With the aerial inserted and extended, position the tube so that it stands slightly proud of the body surface. Check that the aerial is vertical, then tack weld the tunnel in place (4). Immediately after final welding, cool the area with a wet rag to stop the heat from distorting the panel, then file off the excess weld using a small, round hand file. Clean the surrounding area and spread some plastic filler around the hole, blending it in roughly with the contour of the panel. Final shaping can be carried out with a flat metal file (5). When the tunnel is flush with the bodywork, use successively finer grades of abrasive paper until you are left with a smooth overall finish. De-grease the entire area and lay down two coats of primer/surfacer (6).

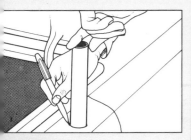

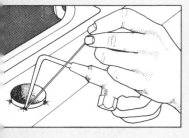

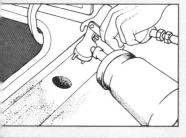

Louvres

One of the more colourful trends to have surfaced in recent years is the 'nostalgia rod/custom'. Many enthusiasts are building cars from scratch to look exactly as though they were built back in the fifties. An essential feature of the heydays' look is the punching of small vents within body panels, or louvring. A fairly simple modification that can add real eye-appeal when applied to the right area(s).

Louvres were first exploited by the early salt lake racers of Southern California. They were punched in hood panels, deck lids, in fact almost anywhere to help relieve air pressure when travelling at high speeds. They also held a psychological advantage in that the car with the most louvres simply looked faster.

Louvred panels soon became commonplace on all types of street driven machinery. Whilst basically emulating the competition look, they were meticulously applied to be aesthetically pleasing. The most common application was on hood panels, although many customizers/rodders punched turret tops, fenders and even skirts for 'street' originality.

If you think that louvres will add style to your machine, be it anything from a model 'T' to an off-road pick-up, you'll have to find a specialist firm to do the work. The actual process is quite simple, but an expensive press is required to punch out the series of vents. These can vary from 2 inches (5cms) to 12 inches (30cms) in width, although not all firms carry the full range of necessary tools.

The subject panel is positioned between male and female dies which are then forced together under great pressure. When one side of the area is raised and the other is lowered, the pressure tears the metal and forms the familiar aperture. The dies have an edge that ensures equal spacing between the louvres. The rows are kept straight and at the desired angle to

the edge of the panel by means of an adjustable guide bar.

All you have to do is decide exactly where you want the series and in what form and length. The only limitation being, whether the intended panel will fit into the press. Flat or single curved panels are easily punched, providing the louvres are to be situated within 12 inches (30cms) of the outside edge. Although, if you're prepared to search hard enough, you may find a firm with tooling that will accommodate panels over this length.

Alternatively, you will have to weld, or rivet, a louvred length of sheet metal into a cut-out in the panel. This method also applies to double curved panels, and those where a reverse-side support makes punching unfeasible. Positioning and size of louvres is obviously a personal choice and one which holds countless possibilities.

Roof chop

A lowered roofline is probably the most direct route to a more stream-lined, purposeful-looking rod or custom. However, it is also one of the most difficult aspects of customizing to complete successfully.

Basically, it involves cutting the desired amount out of the roof and door pillars, then welding the sections back together. This is relatively easy on early vertical struc-tured cars of the twenties and thirties, since all you're doing is lowering the rectangle that the side view presents. Problems start to arise when chopping later cars with tapered and raked pillars, and curved glass. Pillars misalign and skilful metalworking/welding is required to section and re-join the roof. Glass cutting is also more difficult.

'Hammering the lid' of any car is invariably far easier in theory than in practice, so consider carefully what is involved; welding skills, time, patience, an assistant, tools etc., before you attempt anything — otherwise your custom project may end up as a pile of unusable panels.

The basic method

Since you'll be using a high temper-ature welding flame, your first task will be to remove all the interior trim, to eliminate any possibility of fire. Early cars will have a structural wooden framework, which serves as both support for the trimming and stiffening for the body itself. This should be removed from the roof and pillars, but left in place else-where to stop the body from flexing

1 Scribe parallel cut lines around each pillar.

2 Cut accurately along topmost lines.

3 Remove the lid.

4 Cut desired amount from each pillar.

5 Remove paint and imperfections with grinder.

6 Use a jig saw to section the roof.

7 Tack weld each section to appropriate pillar.

8 Clamp sections toget-her across gaps.

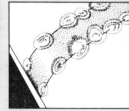
9 Fill roof gaps with sheet metal strips.

10 Tapered edges will require metalwork.

11 Use off-cuts to 'stretch' door frames.

12 Apply plastic filler where necessary.

'Lemon Squash' — a radically chopped '61 Ford Consul Mk11.

when the roof is cut off. Further to this, make sure the car is parked on level ground, and the body is securely bolted to the chassis. Obviously, all the window glass and channels should be removed, along with the doors (if the hinges are located above the intended cutting points). If you own a modern car in which the door window frames are bolted into the door itself, they can be removed and lowered into the skin after the completed roof chop.

Deciding exactly where to cut the roof pillars is the next step. On very early cars, the centre section of each pillar will be both parallel and vertical, making re-alignment quite straightforward. However, later models will require more thought as the supporting structures are generally more complex in design. Your parallel cutting lines will have to be made well below the upper curved portions of the door frames, within the 'straightest' areas of the pillars.

To mark up your lines, select a strip of steel or wood slightly longer than the distance between the front and rear pillars, and of equal width to the required chop. Position it against the pre-determined cutting area and use a spirit level to ensure it is exactly horizontal — an assistant may be necessary. With the strip held or clamped firmly in position, scribe parallel lines on each pillar (1). Measure the distance between the top line and a fixed point, say the gutter, transfer this 'marker' to the other side of the car and repeat the operation as before. You can then scribe continuation lines around each pillar, as a hacksawing guide, using a suitably accurate template. All cut lines will then be parallel and equidistant.

Before cutting, check to see if the inner and outer pillar skins are spot welded between the lines. If they are, drill the welds out, then use a hammer and chisel to carefully separate the two.

Start by making clean, accurate cuts along the topmost line of each pillar, using a hacksaw fitted with a sharp new blade (2). Cut the outer and inner skins separately and have a second person on hand to relieve

the pressure of the roof. When you have completed the upper cuts, remove the 'lid' (3). You can then work your way round the car lowering each pillar by the desired amount (4). Change blades as often as necessary and keep all the off-cuts for final patching.

Now use a small grinder, or an electric drill fitted with a grinding disc, to remove all traces of paint and any imperfections from the pillar stubs (5). A light touch will ensure precise mating of the upper and lower pieces, but take care not to bear down too hard or you'll end up with a roof that is lopsided.

As previously mentioned, if your car incorporates slanting supporting structures you'll have to section the roof, re-join each piece to its appropriate pillar, and fill the resulting gaps with sheet steel. The sectioning will depend on the structure of the car and the number of pillars in question. For example, most late model pick-ups incorporate four slanting pillars, therefore the roof must be quartered.

Use thin masking tape to mark out the roof cutting lines. They don't have to be precisely located, but they must be dead straight and at right angles to each other. Drill a 3/8 inch (9mm) hole where the lines intersect and cut along each one with a jig saw, stopping about 3–4 inches (7.5–10cms) from the outer edges (6). Use a hacksaw to complete the cuts through the flimsy steel. Again, clean up the edges of each roof section to remove any paint and small irregularities prior to re-alignment.

Take one of the rear sections and match it with the appropriate pillar so that the two edges mate together perfectly. Clamp them in position, then make a final check with a straight edge before tack welding (7). Follow the same procedure until all the sections are tacked in place. You can then clamp the sections together across the gaps in the door and window frames using pieces of tubing and steel strips, making certain that everything aligns as it should (8). Before you go any further support the roof with some sort of

prop(s) to prevent it caving in.

Now you can start to fill the gaps. This will involve shaping strips of sheet metal to duplicate the form and contour of the pillar edges, roof panels etc., then tack welding them in place (9, 10). Wherever possible use the original off-cuts within areas such as door jambs or window frames. Also, it's advisable to leave the awkward areas slightly low, relying more on plastic filler for a perfect finish.

When all the filler strips are tacked in position, you can commence final welding. Use a technique known as 'hammer welding' as far as possible. It is best applied to this type of work, that is, where heat distortion must be avoided and utmost strength is required. This two-man operation involves welding the gaps between each tack at alternate spots, then hammering the welds flat whilst they are still red-hot, using a panel beater's hammer and dolly.

Before final finishing, turn your attention to the door window frames. Like the roof pillars, they should be cut within their straightest portions using the same marking method. Unless the car is vertical, they will also have to be 'stretched' to match the longer roof. You can do this by cutting the top of the frame in half, rejoining the side posts, then filling the resultant gap with one of the off-cuts (11).

When all the welds have cooled down, grind them flush and apply plastic filler as required (12). File, sand and re-fill until the joins are no longer visible. Finish off by spraying the various areas with several coats of primer/surfacer, block sanding between each coat to work out the minute low spots.

All that remains is to refit the glass. Most early cars were fitted with flat, toughened glass which cannot be cut — in which case you'll have to make up accurate cardboard templates and take them to a glass specialist, who will cut a new set from laminated glass. The only way to get a modern laminated screen to fit is to cut down the original, which is again specialist work.

Paintwork

No matter how much work you put into modifying or building a car, the paint job is the final touch and the first thing to catch the onlooker's attention.

It is common belief that only professional sprayers possess the mystic talent needed to perform a custom paint job. This is not true.

Many of the top show prizes are awarded to amateurs, whose enthusiasm, coupled with time and patience, has more than compensated for their lack of experience.

The main thing to remember before you apply any primer or paint is that the finished job will only be as good as the surface beneath it, and the key to success lies within a good preparation. Your most essential requirements are a thorough, systematic approach and a keen eye towards perfection from start to finish.

Equipment & work area

The most important tool in auto spraying is the spray gun. It is used in conjunction with a compressor and a regulator. The compressor feeds pressurised air, while the regulator controls the amount of air entering the gun.

Unless you intend doing several paint jobs, it does not make economic sense to buy a brand new spray gun and compressor. It's wiser to hire the equipment from a local hire shop or hunt around for a good secondhand set up. Don't be

separate passages and are mixed, or atomised, and ejected at the air cap.

Air is fed in from the compressor via the air inlet and its volume is controlled by the air valve. Paint is sucked into the gun from the reservoir by the vacuum created at the fluid tip. The function of this device is to control the flow of paint, which it does by means of the orifice size. The fluid needle inside the fluid tip starts and stops the flow of paint. There is also an adjustment control to limit the flow of paint, and this is done by limiting the movement of the fluid needle.

The flow of compressed air is directed by the air cap, which is the nozzle, and it is on this that atomisa-

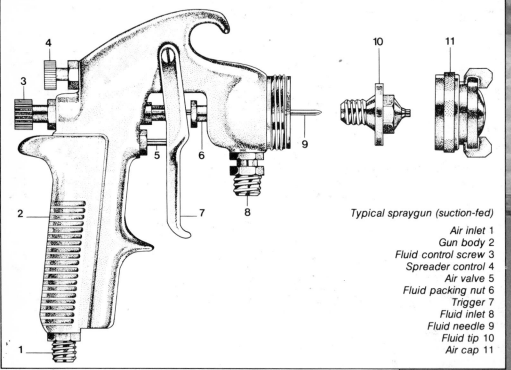

Typical spraygun (suction-fed)

Air inlet 1
Gun body 2
Fluid control screw 3
Spreader control 4
Air valve 5
Fluid packing nut 6
Trigger 7
Fluid inlet 8
Fluid needle 9
Fluid tip 10
Air cap 11

tempted by the cheaper, down market spray guns. You can only hope for the best results if you use good equipment. The most popular type of spray gun used in custom work is an external mix, suction fed gun, where the paint is suspended in a reservoir beneath it. This is the best gun to use for applying fast drying lacquer, although it is suitable for almost all types of automotive paint. Air and paint enter the gun through

tion, as well as the size and shape of the spray pattern, depends. Both the air valve and the fluid needle are operated by the trigger. The other adjuster is the spreader control, which determines the amount of air passing to the holes in the air cap, and thus shapes the paint fan.

Air compressors come in a wide range of shapes, sizes and capacities. They are rated according to their output of air, which is mea-

sured in c.f.m. (cubic feet per minute). The pressure needed to move the air is measured in p.s.i.(pounds per square inch). Your compressor must supply enough air to feed the gun you intend to use, otherwise the pressure may drop as you are spraying and cause an irregular flow of paint. Therefore it is advisable to use a large compressor where the air pressure can be regulated.

An air rectifier, or separator, is used to regulate the air supply. As well as maintaining the correct pressure, it will separate any moisture from the air flow that would otherwise enter the gun, contaminate the paint, and leave tiny craters or blisters in your finished surface. The separator is fitted with a pressure dial and an adjustment knob, by which the required pressure can be set.

Your working area should be clean and well ventilated. Ideally, it will allow you enough room to manoeuvre easily, that is, at least 3 feet (1 metre) all the way round the car. Cramped spraying conditions can be very frustrating as well as highly impractical.

As paint fumes are very dangerous, there should be as much ventilation as possible, without causing a draught. You should always wear a gauze mask when spraying for the same reason.

Whatever the conditions, your main enemy will be dust. Before you start spraying make sure everything is clean. Sweep out all the dirt, and damp the walls and floor with water as a further precaution. Never neglect this chore, otherwise dust may contaminate the paint.

The ideal temperature when spraying is around 65 degrees farenheit. Slightly below will not make a great deal of difference, the paint will just take longer to dry. Avoid spraying in damp, humid, or really cold weather conditions as it may have adverse effects on the finish. The temperature can be raised by using strategically placed electric heaters in the area, but never too close to your car. Avoid using blower heaters as they will stir up the dust.

Preparation

Unless the existing paintwork is in a very poor overall condition, it is rarely necessary to strip it off completely. If stripping is required a chemical paint stripper will make the work a lot easier, although these should never be used in unventilated areas, or on glass fibre.

If the paintwork is in a reasonably good condition for sanding down, you'll need to know what type of paint it is and whether it will be compatible with the fresh layers you intend to put over it. The reason being that if cellulose it sprayed over enamel, or acrylic lacquer over enamel or cellulose, or vice-versa, the new paint may crack, lift or blister and you'll be back to square one. The original top coat must always be sealed if you intend using a different form of paint, or even if you will be spraying the same type of paint over a strong colour, such as red or maroon, which will invariably bleed through.

The factory paint code will be stamped on an identification plate, usually located somewhere on the engine bay. Your local paint suppli will have all the relevant records. you are in any doubt concerning th origin of the existing paint, put small drop of lacquer thinner on th inner door edge. If the paint soften it is lacquer.

For a professional job, carefu unscrew, unbolt and prize up an removable trim, such as light bumpers, radiator grille, nam badges, door rubbers, etc. This w enable the entire bodywork receive paint protection. You will doubt be surprised by the amount grease, wax and less noticeabl

corrosion discovered around light surrounds or side trim.

You will already have straightened out any bodywork imperfections (see Making Good) and the bodywork must now be thoroughly washed and dried. This will remove any debris that may get trapped in the abrasive paper during the sanding process, and cause deep scratch marks in the surface.

Sanding

Using 320 grit wet paper wrapped around a rubber block, and plenty of soapy water, begin sanding each panel. Start with the roof, then

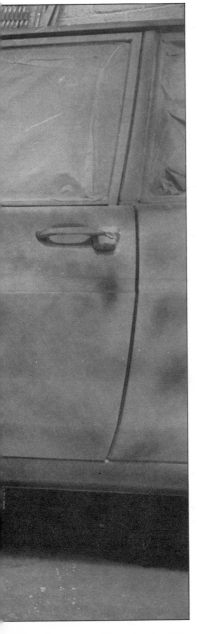

systematically work round the car, taking great care not to over-sand previously filled and primed areas. As you finish one area, use the edge of the rubber block to remove all the excess water, and check that the surface has a uniform matt appearance. You may encounter a number of minor chips and scratches around the lower body panels. These rust spots should be sanded back to bare metal using a coarser paper, and 'feathered' smooth with the surrounding paintwork. Time and patience will be needed for good preparation and it is important not to neglect the more inaccessible areas if you hope to achieve a professional looking finish.

After washing with fresh water, dry the car and blow off any excess dust using compressed air. Clean the entire surface with a de-greasing solvent, working it well into the door hinges with a 1 inch (25mm) paintbrush. As well as removing any surface contamination, the solvent will help provide a good key for subsequent layers of primer and paint.

Masking

The first rule in masking is simple — always use a good quality tape that sticks firmly. Inferior tape will often cause great disappointment when it is lifted from a finished job and you find that paint has crept beneath carefully masked lines. Tapes are available in a variety of widths from 1/8 inch (3mm) upwards, but standard 3/4 inch (18mm) width should be sufficient for a complete re-spray where no intricate design masking is required.

Begin by masking any remaining trim, making sure that the tape does not overlap onto the adjacent body panel. Always press down the edge of the tape with your thumb to ensure good adhesion. Protect the front and rear screens by masking the outer rubbers with short lengths of overlapping tape. Cover the remaining area of glass with strips of

(Left:) Block sanding the dust coat of black with grade 400 wet paper results in a perfectly prepped surface.

brown masking paper. To ensure complete protection from overspray, tape down the edges of the paper firmly. If you intend spraying the inner door jambs, remember to protect the interior by masking the door gaps. You will also need to seal the windows on the inside as well as the outside. If the lower rain gutters are to be sprayed, the inner trunk area and engine compartment should also be well protected. Cover the wheels with clean, fluff-free cloths or polythene. Don't try to cover too much ground too quickly — accurate masking takes time, and any corner-cutting at this stage will show in the end result.

Priming

If you have by-passed the sanding stage by using a paint stripper, treat the bare metal with a chemical rust inhibitor as soon as possible. You can then apply a light coat of etching primer — this will penetrate into the pores of the metal and promote good adhesion.

If you intend using a different type of paint, apply a coat of non-sanding sealer. The prepared surface can then be covered with a good quality primer/surfacer that is compatible with your new top coat. Use an acrylic primer/surfacer for an acrylic lacquer top coat, and so on. This will fill any minor scratches and provide a firm base for further paint coats. Follow the manufacturers' mixing instructions and apply three coats, allowing at least 30 minutes between each. The surface can then be left to shrink and dry for 24 hours.

Next, spray a light mist coat of black primer over the primer/surfacer. This will act as a guide to sanding as it will remain in any low spots or imperfections that may have been previously overlooked.

Block sand with 400 grit paper used with soapy water until the black guide coat disappears and the surface is perfectly smooth. If you happen to go through to bare metal, apply some more primer/surfacer to the area and re-sand. Any irregularities should be filled with putty. When the entire surface is flawless, wash, dry and de-grease ready for the finishing paint coats.

Paints & application

Whatever type of paint and colour you choose, buy enough to do the whole job first time round. Different batches of paint can often vary slightly in colour, so it's advisable to have some over for any minor repairs in the future. One gallon of paint is usually sufficient for the average-sized auto.

it an immediate sheen when dry. However, a surface that has been sprayed in acrylic enamel can take up to eight months to fully harden. You can add special hardeners to the paint that will cut this time down considerably, as well as increasing the life expectancy by 50 per cent, but at the same time this has one distinct disadvantage. Whereas normal acrylic enamel is dust resistant in one hour, the hardener will increase this time to four hours. You should always wear a cartridge type respirator if you spray with the

measure the depth by standing a steel rule upright in the container. For instance, if the depth reads 4 inches (10cms) and the correct dilution is one part paint and one and a half parts diluter, you'll add the diluter until the total level reaches 10 inches (25cms) (2). You can then stir the mixture thoroughly.

The diluted paint should then be strained as you pour it into the paint cup, using a proper paint strainer (3). This will trap any foreign matter that may otherwise block up the gun or contaminate the painted surface.

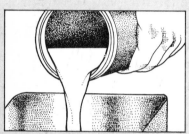

1 *Pour paint into a clean container.*

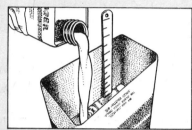

2 *Measure the depth with a steel rule.*

3 *Strain the diluted paint.*

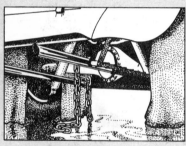

4 *Damp floor and hang a chain from the rear axle to the ground.*

5 *Wipe entire surface with a tack rag.*

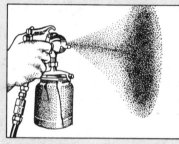

6 *Adjust spreader control to achieve a flat, vertical oval spray pattern.*

There are many different types of paint available for automotive refinishing, although custom sprayers, both amateur and professional, usually favour acrylic lacquer as their medium. This plastic-based material is applied in thin, light coats, slowly building up a durable surface for maximum gloss. Its quick drying characteristics make it ideal if you are not working in dust-free conditions. It also has excellent colour retention.

Enamel paint is much slower drying, and the correct spray pressure and paint dilution are critical if you hope to achieve a successful job. The basic ingredient in any enamel paint is varnish, which gives

added hardener.

Before you apply any paint it must be correctly diluted to ensure an effective spraying consistency. Thinner is used to dilute lacquer, while reducer is used with enamel. Always follow the manufacturers' advice on which thinner or reducer to use and the correct mixing ratio. This will depend a lot on the weather conditions. For example, on a hot dry day, when the paint will dry quickly, you should use a slow drying diluter to compensate.

To dilute the paint, pour three litres into a clean, parallel-sided container (1). An old thinners' can with the top cut off is ideal. Stir the paint well, especially if it is metallic, and

Damp the floor, and hang a chain or something similar from the rear axle to the ground to counteract static which is a further cause of dust attraction (4). Just before you start spraying, wipe the entire surface with a 'tack rag' to remove any dust (5).

Turn up the line pressure to 45 p.s.i. for acrylic lacquer or 65 p.s.i. for acrylic enamel. Test spray an old panel or wall, holding the gun about 10 inches (25cms) from the surface and at right angles to it. Adjust the spreader control until you have a flat vertical oval spray pattern (6), and when you feel satisfied that the paint is flowing smoothly you'll be ready to start the real thing.

If the door, hood and trunk shuts are to be painted, these should be sprayed first, allowed to dry, then shut tight. Treat each exterior panel separately, beginning with the roof area. Start at the front door pillars and work backwards and try to get a flat, even distribution of paint. Maintain a constant distance between the gun and surface and never swing the gun in an arc across the panel as this will cause dry spots at the end of each pass. Each sideways pass should overlap the previous one by 50 per cent. You should also 'trigger-off' at the end of every pass to avoid overspray and a heavy build-up of paint around the edges.

After spraying the roof and door pillars move to the hood. Start at the top and work right down to the lower balance area. Spray the left fender, then move to the right. Finish off the entire right side, to the edge of the rear fender. Come back round to the left side, finishing off at the trunk.

If this is your first attempt at spray painting, you may be inclined to start at one point and work straight round the car. This method will make it very difficult to blend in the final panel with the first, as the paint will be almost dry by the time you reach your original starting point.

Using the correct spray pattern, you will need to apply either three coats of acrylic enamel or five coats of acrylic lacquer for a good finish. The safe drying time between each coat will depend on the weather conditions. Fifteen minutes should suffice, but always allow a while longer in cold weather. For a nice glossy finish, spray the final coat fairly 'wet', that is, apply more paint.

When you finish spraying, let the paint dry before peeling off any masking. This means at least one hour for lacquer, and three hours for enamel. If the surface looks good, remove the tape slowly, taking great care not to peel away any paint.

Few amateurs achieve a perfect finish first time. Don't worry, many of the minor faults can be easily rectified without having to start all over again. If, after drying, your surface shows signs of dust and dirt, you should lightly sand the affected areas with 1200 wet paper. Rub the paper against a bar of soap to help obtain a smooth, flat surface. The fine scratch marks can then be rubbed out with compound, and waxed for a gloss finish. The same method can be used to rectify minor runs, sags and 'orange peel'.

Runs or sags are usually caused by piling on heavy or 'wet' coats of paint. 'Orange peel' is a common fault, where the surface resembles the skin of an orange. The usual causes are a wrong nozzle adjustment and spraying technique, or incorrect dilution. If the entire surface is marred by orange peel, it's better to flat it down and respray, using more diluter.

Bad preparation is often responsible for faults in the finish. Incorrect feathering will cause deep indentations. Grease or wax on the surface prior to spraying may lead to tiny pin holes. The only remedy in these cases is to sand the areas, apply more primer, and repaint.

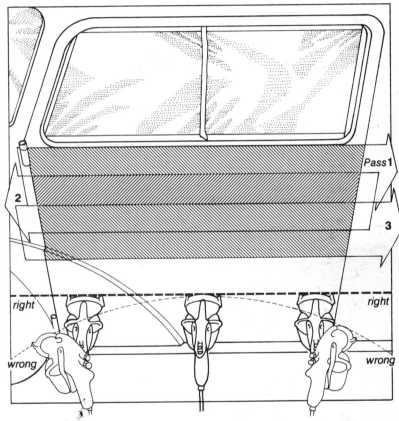

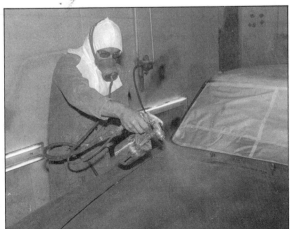

Above: Diagram shows how each sideways pass should overlap the previous one by 50%. Try to maintain a constant distance of 8 - 10ins. (20 - 25cms) between gun and surface.

Left: Always wear a cartridge respirator when spraying acrylic enamel with added hardener.

KPU 717J

Left: Mercury leadsled is entitled 'So Fine'. What more can be said about this candy apple dream? *Lower left:* A rich, single tone paint scheme will enhance the 'genuine' feel of an early rod. This one has great, high lacquered depth. *Centre:* Re-shaped Ford Capri incorporates just about every conceivable trick paint technique. *Lower right:* Vans provide a lot of space for creativity. Early Fordson exploits a complex design which, through careful use of colour, produces a very tasteful overall effect.

Custom paints

Candy

Candy colours are tinted transparent acrylic lacquers. They can give varying effects, depending on which base colour you choose and how many candy coats you lay over it. You can apply any colour you like as a base, although those most widely used are white, white pearl, or the metallic range (gold, silver or bronze) because of their highly reflective quality. A gold metallic base will give a fiery brilliance underneath any candy. Silver will 'chrome' the overall effect, while bronze gives a rich, warm tone. With a little forethought on colour mixing, some very interesting results can be achieved. For example, a yellow base covered with candy blue will produce a greenish-blue top colour.

Whatever base colour you choose, it must be applied evenly all over. Any imperfection will be highlighted by the candy and may ruin the overall effect. With a metallic base, remember to agitate the spray gun after every couple of strokes in order to keep the particles dispersed. If the base needs sanding down, use 600 wet paper and lightly 'coloursand' the surface with continuous strokes in the same direction. Sand horizontally on the sides, and vertically on the hood, roof and deck lid. After washing and drying, de-grease the car and try not to touch it again.

When you have achieved a solid base colour, free of all lumps and uneven abrasions, you will be ready to apply the candy. It should be mixed in the ratio of 1 part candy to 1½/2 parts lacquer thinner. Spray 15—18 inches (37—45cms) from the surface using 70/75 p.s.i. As the overall colour becomes deeper with successive coats, it is important that you spray each layer evenly to avoid darker or lighter patches. You can achieve this evenness by using an alternate spray pattern over the car. One stroke horizontally, the next vertically and then diagonally in both directions. Never stop and start at the same point as this will cause nasty streaks. Any runs you might get cannot be sanded down, so always spray thin, dry layers, building up the density slowly. As a further precaution, wait at least fifteen minutes between each coat. When you've reached the desired effect, stop there. Too many coats will eventually dull the reflective base and lessen the true candy effect.

As soon as the final coat has dried, spray three or four coats of clear acrylic lacquer to seal the candy against dust, dirt or any other marks. If necessary, wait about a month before coloursanding with 1200 wet paper. Use compound and wax for a deep gloss finish.

Flake

Flake paint can give any car a very distinctive, shimmering appearance. It consists of tiny mylar particles, mixed and suspended in clear acrylic lacquer or candy, and applied over a corresponding base colour. These highly reflective particles are sold in packet form in a variety of brilliant colours and sizes. Before you invest in the largest size, check that they will flow through the spray gun that you will be using.

Although you will aim for maximum flake coverage, there will invariably be tiny gaps between some of the particles. Your base will serve as a 'colour safety shield' between the flake and bare body primer. It should be prepared to the same extent as a candy base. No dark or light patches, runs or streaks. Alternatively you can use one of the manufacturers' specially coloured primer/surfacers during the body preparation stage.

The clear acrylic lacquer should first be thinned 1½ to 1 with lacquer thinner. To mix the flake, pour the thinned lacquer into the paint cup, stopping about 1½ inches (3.75cms) from the top. Drop in a couple of clean ball bearings or nuts, which will help to disperse the flake when agitated. Add just under 2oz. (57g) of dry flake and stir the mixture vigorously. Test spray the mixture on an old panel, using a low pressure of 25 p.s.i. The flake will bounce off the surface if you use a high pressure application. If the flake seems too sparse add a little more.

Spray the car using the candy technique and criss-crossing consecutive strokes. After four or five coats you should have a sufficiently even coverage and the desired effect. To obtain a smooth finished surface, spray as many coats of clear lacquer as necessary.

Pearl

Pearl is probably among the most subtle of all custom finishes. It is applied over a base colour in the same way as candy and flake.

In certain lights, a car painted in pearl will contain brilliant, two tone changes of colour on the curves and highlights. The most expensive pearl paints are made from herring scales that have been ground down into a fine powder and mixed with paste. Synthetic pearl, made of lead-salt crystals, will give a similar effect at a much lower cost.

It is available in various colours, such as red, green, blue, gold and platinum, but they all have a milk white appearance in the can. Their effects differ tremendously according to the base colour you choose, e.g., a red pearl over a white base will stay basically white, but will give a slightly red tint in the highlights and a green cast in the shadows. Red pearl over a black base will produce a bright red finish that has brilliant lustre. Over a dark blue base, the highlights will be red, the shadows blue/purple and the flat panels green/orange, when viewed from an acute angle in half light.

Pearl comes in liquid concentrate or powdered form and is mixed with thinned, clear acrylic lacquer. Use a slow drying thinner to allow the crystals to flow and settle before drying. Never spray too many coats as you will lose the pearlescent effect. Pearls can be mixed with candies for a heightened colour effect and a unique custom paint job.

Using an airbrush

An airbrush is a sophisticated miniature spray gun, capable of delivering fine, adjustable patterns of paint. It is used mostly for murals and lettering, where fine detailed work is called for. Commercial artists have been using the airbrush for a long time, and it remains the most versatile tool for creating three dimensional painted images on a two dimensional surface.

Like its full-size relative, the airbrush must have a source of compressed air, to atomise the paint as it goes through the nozzle. If you are planning to do a lot of airbrush work it's worth investing in a portable compressor. Alternatively, you can buy a handy 20oz. (567g) aerosol can that should last long enough for a small mural. It's advisable to use a regulator valve with the can as this will allow you to reduce the pressure and obtain greater control with the spray widths.

There are two basic types of airbrush available to use with automotive paint; the single action, or the more expensive double action. A needleless single action airbrush is capable of spraying heavy paints, even metalflake, from a 4 inch (10cms) pattern down to a ½ inch (12mm) width. It has a button that controls the volume of air and a separate adjustment screw for the volume of paint. This entails a skilful two handed operation.

A needle-controlled, single action airbrush is easier to operate and will spray fine lines of 1/16 inch (1.5mm) width. It is also very useful for multi-coloured mural work as it will utilize different sized paint reservoirs.

The double action airbrush is perhaps the best all-purpose applicator. It has one button that controls both paint and air volume — therefore it can be used with one hand when spraying. Air flow is increased by pushing the button down, and paint flow by pulling it back. Pushing down and pulling back at the same time will increase the spray volume and broaden the spray pattern.

Before you attempt any work on your car, first get the feel of the tool and its capabilities. Build up darker tones with overlapping passes (1) and practise straight and curved lines of varying widths (2). Draw out three dimensional boxes and fill in the appropriate shadows and highlights (3 and 4). Become familiar with the correct distances between airbrush and surface, at different pressures, until you feel confident enough to tackle the real thing.

If you are spraying with acrylic lacquer, you should dilute the paint more than usual, the reason being that it dries very rapidly in small quantities and may clog the airbrush, producing a splattering effect. It's a good idea to keep a separate reservoir of thinner to spray through the tool in between changing colours. As it is a precision instrument, minute particles of dried paint will affect its future use. You should always dismantle and thoroughly clean the components with thinner after every job, taking care not to lose or damage any parts.

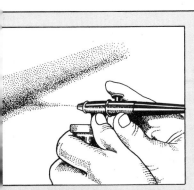

1 *Build up darker tones with overlapping passes.*

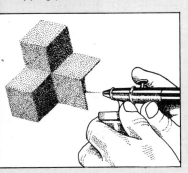

2 *Practise straight and curved lines of varying widths.*

3 *Fill in the appropriate shadows...*

4 *...and highlights.*

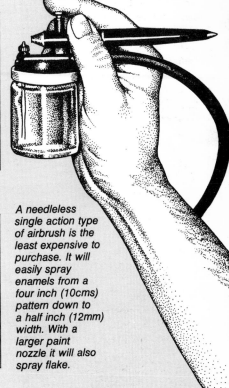

A needleless single action type of airbrush is the least expensive to purchase. It will easily spray enamels from a four inch (10cms) pattern down to a half inch (12mm) width. With a larger paint nozzle it will also spray flake.

Techniques

Having applied the overall colour to your car, you may now wish to embellish it further, using one or a number of 'trick techniques'. Before you apply any pinstripes, flames or fish scales, carefully consider whether or not they will enhance the 'image' of your machine. A few tasteful additions will often look far superior and take much less time than an 'all out' attack on your car.

Pinstriping

The art of pinstriping can be used to enhance the natural, flowing lines or favourable features of your car. It will also add a very 'finished' look to the edges of flames, lettering or contrasting panels. As with all custom-painting techniques, there are no definite rules on its use or over-use.

You can create unique designs by hand striping with a fine camel hair brush. Alternatively, there are a number of adhesive tapes and transfers available that can be used very effectively. Whichever method you choose, it's a good idea to pencil out all your ideas first on a sheet of paper.

If you intend doing the job by hand you'll need the appropriate brushes. A flat handled 'dagger' brush is used for straight pulls, whilst a round handled 'sword' is best for curves. These can be obtained from art stores in sizes 00.0 and 1. The most suitable paint is synthetic enamel, as used by signwriters. It will cover in one coat and dry slowly, allowing time to rectify any mistakes.

Flaming

Alongside pinstriping, flame painting is the oldest custom technique still practised today. Flames can radiate from the front, sides or wheels of your car. Long and flowing, short or stubby, single or multi-coloured. They come in all shapes and sizes

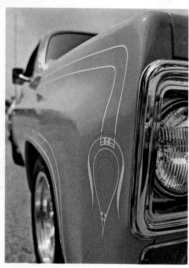

...nd can be used to create varying effects. A traditional red and yellow flame job will add a visual feeling of power and performance to almost any car, whereas a slight change in colour tone between body and frames can produce a very subtle 'speed' effect.

Panels and decorations

If you are aiming towards a contrast of colours and effects, it is best to confine the treatment to 'panels'. The idea is to mask out certain areas that will either compliment or disguise the overall shape of your car. What you do within these panels is entirely up to you.

Obvious situations for panel painting are doors, hood, fenders and deck lid. You could, for instance, divide the whole side of the car into two panels. A long, narrow upper panel running the entire length of the car, and a wider lower panel covering the distance between the inner edges of the wheel arches.

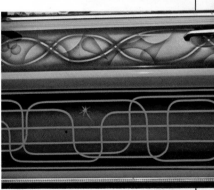

Pinstriping

Prior to paint application, soak the brush for a few minutes in a saucer of turpentine. This will clean and soften it, ready for working. The right consistency of paint and turps is critical if you hope to achieve good free flowing lines. Hold the brush between thumb and forefinger, using the other fingers as a guide (1). Practise straight lines and varying curves on a piece of glass or an old body panel in order to gain confidence (2 and 3). Always apply a constant pressure for a consistent line thickness. The usual way of ending a line is to let it taper to a fine point, although 'arrow heads' and 'feather tips' can look exciting (4). Experiment with contrasting colours and combinations of stripes until you feel certain that you have the best effect for your car.

1

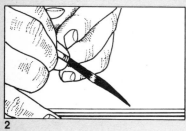

2

3

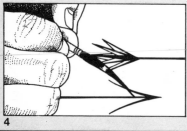

4

Flaming

Use a chinagraph pencil to outline the shape of the flames (1). If the body is a dark colour you'll need to use a white grease pencil. The flames don't have to be exactly symmetrical, but try to get the curves very round and the points very sharp for an acceptable result. Keep persisting until you are satisfied that the design is 'just right'. Now you are ready to mask the edges of the flames with ⅛ inch (3mm) masking tape, making sure that it is firmly stuck, especially around the tight curves (2). Protect all the areas not to be painted with brown masking paper (3). Try to plan the work so that the tape is not left on overnight, for if it gets damp you may have difficulty removing it.

Using a fine dry paper, sand the entire flame area, taking great care not to scuff the crisp edge of the masking tape. To eliminate the sealing and priming process, choose a compatible paint for your base. Spray the 'overall' colour first and leave it to dry. You can then blend or fog darker shades and contrasting colours over it. Always remember to put down light, dry coats of paint, otherwise you'll be left with a distinct 'ridge' between the flames and body. If you're working in lacquer, de-grease the car and apply several coats of clear for protection. A fine pinstripe will add the finishing touch to your flame job (4).

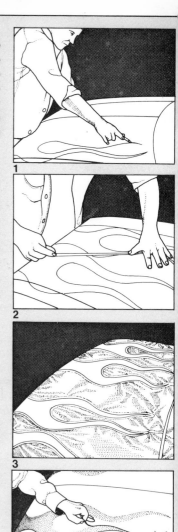

1

2

3

4

Panels and decorations

When masking, always lay down the horizontal lines first. This can be done with ¾ inch (19mm) masking tape. Position a few inches of tape at one end, then unroll the required length, holding it taut. Look along the edge of the tape, making sure it's straight, then lay it down in position. If you are taping over difficult curves, a second person will be needed to apply pressure to the tape at the apex. As you construct the shapes, let all the corners meet at points. You can then use ⅛ inch (3mm) tape to form the required curves. When the panels are successfully masked out, carefully protect the surrounding areas with masking paper.

Fogging

One of the simplest, yet most striking, paint techniques is fogging. It is achieved by directing the centre of a spray pattern at a masked edge so that the paint gradually fades away from it. The paint should be mixed fairly thin and the air pressure dropped to about 35 p.s.i. Always apply light coats, allowing the 'fog' to build up naturally. A fine, base coloured pinstripe running close to the dense edge can look very effective. This is done by laying ⅛ inch (3mm) or ¼ inch (6mm) masking tape parallel to the main panel masking, and ⅛ inch or ¼ inch from it.

Spaghetti stripes

Spaghetti striping is another trick technique using narrow masking tape. As the name suggests, these are free flowing lines which are fogged over, leaving a base coloured stripe. You can create interesting designs by overlapping the stripes and fogging them in different colours.

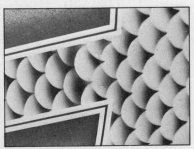

Fish scales

Various patterns can be made by fogging around card masks. A common effect is fish scaling, a repeat pattern that can be carried on indefinitely. To make the mask, pencil out a series of circles, edge to edge, along the side of a piece of square card. The card should be slightly wider than your panel. Cut around the semi-circular shapes with a sharp knife, making sure that the points between the circles are all the same depth. Place the mask flat against the body surface and spray down the edge, using a small fan adjustment. This will produce a series of lightly fogged semi-circular edges. Move the card back and offset it so that the centre of each circle almost touches the sharp points of the previous line, and repeat the fogging. A surface resembling fish scales will gradually appear. Almost any shape of card can be used as a template to produce, what appear to be, very complex panel decorations.

Lace

An extension of the card-masking theme is lace work. You can create intricate effects by stretching lace over a panel, then spraying over it. Convex surfaces are obviously best suited. The lace should be stretched tautly over the panel and taped down either side for good definition. Cotton usually gives a clearer pattern than nylon as well as soaking up the excess paint. Always use a low spray pressure, about 25 p.s.i., to avoid the lace lifting. Two or three light coats should be enough, and never remove the lace until the paint is dry, or it will smudge the surface.

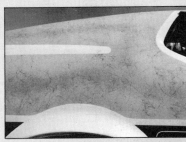

Cobwebbing

'Cobwebbing' is a term that describes long, stringy blobs of paint that are spat out of the gun onto the surface. It is achieved by spraying acrylic paint, mixed with 10 per cent thinners, at a very low pressure of 10–15 p.s.i. The gun should be held about three feet (one metre) from the surface and at 90 degrees to it. This will result in a heavy 'webbing' effect'. You can then adjust the thinning ratio or line pressure to vary the strength of the web. It usually looks most effective when a dark colour is sprayed over a light base.

Before applying any of these techniques to your car, always practise on an old body panel first. Over enthusiasm will often result in great disappointment. Use your imagination to experiment, but, most of all, plan your work carefully for a succsssful 'trick finish'.

Lettering

Lettering is an art form in itself, not to be rushed into. Different letter forms can express different things. For instance, slanting italic letters can suggest speed and motion, whereas bold upright letters create a feeling of strength and stability. Think about the name or title and the way you wish to express it. Consider the shape of your car — is it linear, bulbous, tough or elegant? Your choice of lettering should complement the title, mood and overall appearance of the car.

There are a wide variety of letter forms to choose from, contained in 'type face' catalogues which are available from art stores. Look at magazines, books, posters, or anywhere where lettering appears. You'll soon get the feeling for letter forms and the different effects they can give.

Tracing and enlarging your words

When you have chosen a suitable type face, draw a straight or variable line on a piece of tracing paper. This will act as a base for the letters to sit on. Trace round each letter very accurately, watching the spacing between them (1). They do not have to be an equal distance apart, just concentrate on getting the complete word to look right visually. It will probably take several attempts, so be patient.

If you wish you can now personalize the word(s) further, by adding a shadow or a blocked three dimensional effect, both of which involve the same simple process. First, trace the outline of the completed lettering, so that you have two exact copies. Tape one copy down on a sheet of white paper and place the other directly over it, moving it diagonally up or down (2). The illusion of depth will increase as you move it further away.

When you have found the desired effect, tape the top copy in position and pencil in the bits of lettering that would show through if it was filled in solid (3). For block letters, simply join the shadow to the lettering across the diagonals and fill in the surrounding shapes (4).

The next stage is to enlarge the lettering to the actual size that it will appear on your car. This is achieved by using a 'grid' system. Draw a box around the word(s) and divide it up into equal squares (5). Each square should measure about one quarter of the height of the tallest letter. Then draw an enlarged version of the box to the required size, dividing it up in to the same ratio of squares (6). Working line for line and square for square, you can then pencil in the full-scale lettering (7). You may have to do this transfer process in two or more stages, depending on the required size (8).

Transferring to car and painting
Using 2 inch (5cms) masking tape, mask the entire area where the design will appear. Tape the enlargement in the correct position and draw round the outline (1). Remove the paper leaving the indented shape on the masking tape.

Cut out the non-shadow areas first with a scalpel (2). Key the surface with a fine, dry abrasive paper, then de-grease. Spray the base colour first in thin light coats

(3). You can then add any details such as pinstripes, highlights or fogging. A fine pinstripe around the edges of the letter will visually hold the words to the car (4). Highlights often look effective on rounded letters.

When the paint is dry, you can cut out the shadow areas, mask the completed sections, and repeat the process. After allowing sufficient drying time, unpeel the masking and finish the job with several coats of clear lacquer.

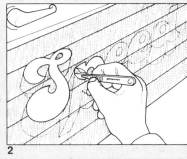

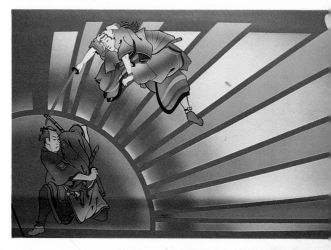

Murals

A tasteful mural can put the final 'icing on your cake'. An imaginative design, whether scenic or abstract, will transform your car into a moving picture story. Murals can emphasize subtlety, style, humour, power or absolutely anything. They should contain something of your own personality and tastes, as well as harmonizing with the shape of the car.

It must be said that most prize winning effects are done by professional muralists who have exceptional artistic ability, but don't let this fact put you off. With a little practice you should be able to achieve a pleasing result that will add new life to your set of wheels.

Mural techniques

The equipment you'll need will be an airbrush, a scalpel and some spare blades, 2 inch (5cm) masking tape and Frisk film. It's a good idea to have a number of extra paint jars for the airbrush, so you can keep all the colours you'll be using ready mixed. This will make a complex job much easier. Frisk film is a clear low-tack film generally used by graphic artists for precise masking. It should only be applied to paintwork that is thoroughly dry, otherwise it will leave behind a residue of glue.

Unless you have a natural ability for creating freehand designs, your first move is to make a full-scale drawing on paper of the intended mural. Leave at least 9 inches (22.5cms) along the top edge.

Simple scenic views or silhouettes are the easiest things to attempt first time. You can use reference from a number of different sources to assemble a unique design. However, it may be necessary to enlarge or reduce certain pieces of reference in order to keep the proportions right. Travel posters often contain excellent material worth tracing off.

The main thing to consider when choosing a mural design is the existing base colour. It should do as much of the work as possible. For instance, a cloudy night scene is best suited to a car that is painted in a dark colour, while a desert scene will blend easily with yellow or sky blue.

Take your drawing, position it centrally and squarely on the chosen panel, and tape it down along the top edge. You can then mask and protect the surrounding area, leaving a 9 inch (22.5cm) bord around the sides and bottom edg This will allow enough space blend the mural colours gently ir the base colour. Fold back t hinged drawing and tape it to t upper panel or window.

Always put the sky colours in fir allowing the natural soft edge of t airbrush spray to determine t beginning and end of your pictu Cloud formations are next and the are best formed using differe shaped paper masks. Tear tl edges of the mask unevenly, th fog in the appropriate colours. Hig light the edges of the clouds using fine spray at low pressure.

With the sky colours complet and dry, use 2 inch (5cm) maskir tape and cover the horizon are Fold down the master drawing ar draw over the horizon line. This w leave a noticeable mark on the tap Lift up the picture and cut along tl line with a sharp scalpel, takir great care not to cut into the pai underneath. Remove the low portion of the tape and protect tl sky area from the horizon and for ground colours. Spray light colou first, then gradually build up th darker tones.

Any other details you may wish include within the mural, such a buildings, vehicles, people etc should be approached individuall First cover the whole mural are with Frisk film, then fold down th master drawing and draw round th outline of the feature. Fold back th drawing and use a fine pen to defin the marks left on the Frisk film Assuming all your paints are mixe and ready, it's simply a question c time, method and patience. Cut ou the segments within the feature tha will be the same colour. Spray th areas, let the paint dry, then stic the pieces of Frisk film back for pro tection. Cut the next segments out spray the next colour, and so on When you've finished all the details remove the Frisk film.

To add any further detailing or fin lines, use a very fine brush or india ink pen. Finish off with several coat of clear lacquer until all the har edges or ridges disappear.

CHP 625K

Care of paintwork

After all the hard work, you'll want to maintain the 'new' image of your custom paint job for as long as possible. Providing you take the necessary precautions, it should last for many years. This will of course depend a lot on where you keep the car. The best place is obviously a garage, where it is relatively sealed against all weather conditions. Harsh sunlight, evening dew, leaf stains, bird lime and the various man-made atmospheric pollutions will all have adverse effects on the surface within a short period of time. This is especially true with heavily lacquered finishes, that are prone to yellowing. If you are not fortunate enough to own a garage, it may be worth investing in a tailor-made plastic cover for your car.

Always clean the body regularly to remove dirt, road film or other acids and chemicals that will encourage rust. First, hose down the car with cold water to remove any loose debris. You can then use one of the specially formulated car shampoos in warm water and gently wash down the paintwork. Don't forget the front and rear valance area. Hose off all the suds, and use a chamois leather to dry the surface, rinsing it regularly in cold water. Any water left on the surface may spot the paint.

If you have an enamel surface, avoid the next stage of polishing and waxing unless the paint is more than six months old, or if it was sprayed with an added hardener that cuts the total drying time down to twenty-four hours. Use a good quality polish with a soft rag and apply it to one panel at a time. Have a separate clean cloth on hand for rubbing the areas to a deep shine. Polish is used to remove the light film of dirt that accumulates with everyday road use. Any bird lime or tar spots can be eliminated with special cleaners and solvents that are designed specifically to remove stubborn marks. Machine polishing is much quicker than hand rubbing, but unless you have experience of using a mechanical cleaner it is very easy to cut right through the paint — so be warned!

After polishing you can seal the newly restored paint with a wax protection. A good waxing will prolong the gloss finish and make it easier to wash off future dirt and debris, without putting tiny scratchmarks in the surface.

Depending on the amount of exposure, the wax should provide protection from three to nine months, and by washing the car periodically you will see when the coating is wearing off. When the water lies in sheets on the surface instead of dispersing into droplets, it will be time to repeat the polish and wax process. If after a period of time the colour shows signs of fading or losing its deep gloss, use a rubbing compound to remove the oxidized paint and bring back the true original colour.

Interiors

The styling you impose on your interior should reflect the overall image you're trying to achieve. For example, if it's the 'gennie resto-rod' feel that you're after, it's more a case of reviving the inside than transforming it. On the other hand you may wish to rid your late model car or van of its moulded plastic panels and re-design in luxurious deep buttoned dralon. Whatever the case, stand back, look and consider — remember it's what you'll see most of.

Upholstery

Upholstery is generally considered to be the one aspect of customizing that's 'best left to the pro's'. However, it's not as difficult as you might think. As long as you approach the work logically and try not to rush things, there is no reason why you shouldn't achieve a professional result. As with any other job, a good eye for detail and lots of patience are the most essential ingredients for success. The tools you'll need will be totally influenced by the work you are going to do, so think carefully before making any purchases.

Equipment and tools

If you intend re-upholstering the whole of your interior, your first consideration should be a sewing machine. An industrial type is strongly recommended as it will make easy work of stitching the heavy materials and carpet used in auto trimming. As they are expensive to buy new, try hunting around the second hand stores and industrial suppliers for a cheap one. Also, it's a good idea to take a sample of the heaviest material you will be working with when you try out a machine. Although many craftsmen prefer to use old fashioned, heavy duty treadle machines, the electric type are quicker and generally easier to handle. Most normal domestic machines are really only suitable for working with light-weight materials. The tension set-up is such that the needle will either bend or snap in two under the strain of material of heavier gauge. Of course, you can always do the job by hand, but this will require much time, patience and skill, especially in those areas where the seams are going to show.

If you are re-designing your seating arrangement, side panels etc., you'll probably have to cut some difficult plywood shapes to serve as backing panels for new upholstery. A jig saw or similar drill attachment will make this job easier.

An upholsterers' ripping chisel is used in conjunction with a mallet for extracting tacks from an existing wooden framework. You can substitute an inexpensive wood chisel or screwdriver for the ripping tool but a mallet will be useful in many situations and is well worth the outlay.

For marking out materials, use a medium that is easily removable. Tailors' chalk is available in a variety of colours and is best used for marking cloths, carpets and other materials. You need only to highlight the line, so pick a colour that is similar to the colour you are working on. Never use black tailors' chalk or a felt tip pen. Black chalk is almost indelible, while a water-based felt tip mark will, with the help of a little perspiration, come through to the surface of the material. A white chinagraph pencil will be very useful when working with a dark vinyl or rubber-backed carpet — it comes off easily with a drop of lighter fuel. But again, never use it on material. Finally, a 'black prince' graphite pencil, as used by carpenters, is ideal for marking up foam.

For accurate cutting, you'll need a good pair of shears and a razor-type knife. Ordinary household scissors are not suitable as they tend to pull threads as they cut. A 'Barnsley' knife is the best tool for trimming off excess material. It has a very sharp, rigid blade, of a length that will enable you to get into awkward areas. Never use a surgical scalpel as excessive pressure will cause the flexible blade to snap and fly off.

A good selection of needles of both bayonet point and round point will be very handy and inexpensive. The button needle is a heavy straight needle, pointed at both ends and triangular in section down one-third of its length. It is used mostly for threading buttons in deep buttoning work. A spring needle is curved and bayonet pointed and is necessary for penetrating tough materials such as leather. Being curved, it's also easier to sew on the back of something as the needle returns in the direction it came from. A half-circular needle is narrower and used for stitching thinner material and/or awkward areas. A 'regulator' incorporates a flat end for pushing material into tight corners.

Upholsterers' skewers may sometimes be needed to hold material temporarily in position.

By tradition, a magnetic tacking hammer is the tool used in mounting upholstery onto wood, as it enables tacks to be driven home without using your fingers as a guide. However, in recent years many trimmers have switched to using the electric or air-powered staple gun. These tools are neat and compact and their protruding end enables quick, easy tacking in almost any situation. Obviously, they are very expensive and not feasible for a one-off job. A cheaper alternative is the manual type normally used in heavy stationery work, although their flush design makes tacking rather tricky in difficult areas. Your best bet is to follow tradition and stick to the slower 'mag' hammer which, for a price well below any low-range staple gun, will give you enough versatility to tackle any job. You'll also need a good supply of tacks and these vary from ⅛ inch to ⅝ inch (3mm to 15mm) in length, although ¼ inch and ⅛ inch (6mm and 3mm) tacks are most frequently used on plywood.

Although hand strength is usually sufficient for stretching material over a particular area, a hide strainer may be necessary for a really tight, pre-tensed finish. It has scored or grooved jaws which clamp the material, while the point of fulcrum enables it to be pulled tight over an edge. However, it must only be used on a hard timber or metal framework/panel. The hardboard panels used in most modern cars will buckle before you achieve the required tautness. Similarly, a web strainer is used to stretch webbing across a hard seat frame. This will be necessary if you intend constructing a new seating arrangement or totally refurbishing an existing item, otherwise it is not essential.

Other DIY items needed are a flexible 6ft (2m) tape for measuring contours, a wooden yardstick for measuring, marking and cutting material and a fine-toothed hacksaw blade for cutting foam.

Materials

The golden rule when choosing materials is to select them according to the work you're doing and buy the best quality you can afford. Upholstering is very time consuming work, so don't use cheap materials that won't wear well, especially on seats. It's wiser to use a lesser quality material within areas such as the headlining.

Leather

Leather is a natural material and as such has many fine qualities, quite apart from a unique character and beauty. It is tough, pliable and, given periodical 'moisturizing' treatment, wears superbly. However, good leather is very expensive, mainly because of the complicated preparation work involved, and it is also difficult to work with, especially if you have ambitious ideas.

It is supplied in hides or half-hides, a hide being the skin of the larger bovine animals such as cows and horses. On average, one skin measures about 50 sq.ft. (16 sq.m.), although there is always some wastage caused by the irregular shape. Moreover, it is difficult to find an unblemished hide free of barbed wire scar marks, small holes or thin patches, so inspect carefully before you buy. As a rough guide, one hide should be enough for two seats.

Apart from the wide range of straight colours available, you can also buy interesting metallic leather — for real trick status!

Suede

Suede is made by splitting a hide in two, or by placing it under a large revolving cylinder covered with an abrasive — hence the familiar texture. Suede is not very practical in a car, especially within those areas that take wear, as it shines quickly and picks up dirt and dust. Nevertheless, it could be used to good effect on a contrasting raised area within a door panel, for example. Like leather, it is both expensive and difficult to work with.

Dralon

Dralon is probably the most popular material for emphasizing the 'luxurious custom upholstery look', particularly when applied to button-ing work. Unlike hide, it has a man-made pile that comes in varying types or grades which are sewn onto a weave backing. Thus you can buy velvet dralon, coarse dralon, nylon dralon and so on. The latter is usually the cheapest, but also the least hard wearing.

When working with any pile material, the pile should be kept running in the same direction all the time, i.e. downwards for the best effect. It is also advisable to double-stitch every seam otherwise the material will have a tendency to fray. Dralon cleans easily with a damp sponge and it will not fade.

Velvet

Proper heavy-duty upholstery velvet is a beautiful material which can produce very tasteful effects. However, given normal everyday treatment, the high gloss finish usually becomes matted all too quickly. It is therefore far from ideal for seats, other than those in show cars. Obviously, if the whole concept is based around pure show, you may wish to use something really wild, such as crushed or sculptured velvet. These materials incorporate multi-directional or patterned pile and can look effectively ostentatious in the right surroundings.

A more practical and less expensive alternative is cord, a ribbed material with a cut pile similar to straight velvet. Accuracy is called for both in cutting and sewing cord in order to keep the ribs running perfectly straight.

Leathercloth and Vinyls

The word 'leathercloth' is often used as a generic term to describe the wide range of imitation leather materials available. Leathercloth itself is actually a plastic material with a woven backing. It does not stretch very well and is really only suitable for covering flat panels, or as a taut headliner.

The expanded vinyls, namely Ambla, Cirrus, Fleximin etc., are a much better choice as upholstery materials. These usually consist of a stretchable, leather-grained PVC surface laminated onto a thin foam base, supported by a woven backing. They have a nice soft feel and are relatively easy to work with. They are available in a variety of colours with embossed grain effects, and some are even variegated to give the 'genuine antique' impression — ideal for resto-rods. They will stretch several inches widthways but not so much lengthways. Easily cleaned and wet-resistant, a high quality vinyl, such as Ambla, makes an excellent substitute for high cost leather.

Naughahyde

Naughahyde is a rather special suede-effect vinyl and a favourite material among American customizers. Although similar in appearance to suede, it is stiffer and has a much thicker feel. It stretches quite well and has superb weather-resistant quality, which explains why it is sometimes found on car exteriors. Another reason for 'hyde being so popular is the fantastic range of colours available, including some wild marble-like effects.

Padding materials

You'll need to use some form of padding under your chosen materials(s) in order to achieve a feeling of comfort and richness. Polyester foam is the most useful material for this purpose. It is supplied in block form in various thicknesses, and is priced in relation to its density. High density foam is best for load bearing applications, i.e. seating, while low density will be adequate in most other areas. As a guide to thickness, ½ inch (12mm) is most suitable on flat door panels, 2 inch (5cm) for buttoning, while 3 or 4 inch (7.5 or 10cm) is usual on a scratch-built seat frame, although expensive thick-core rubber latex foam is sometimes preferred.

Block foam is useful where a more rigid shape/supporting strength is required, e.g. the vertical edge of a seat. It consists of rubber foam chips that are glued together.

Finally, a very thin, inexpensive, material called wadding should always be included between foam padding and a non-leather/leathercloth cover material. It stops the two sticking together and pulling when stretched. Wadding is also used for padding out flutes in 'tuck'n'roll.

Deep buttoning

The ultimate in luxurious upholstery must be deep buttoning. The material is supported by a thick foam underlay into which a symmetrical design of buttons are fixed, thus forming deep pleated pockets and a 'rise and fall' surface contour. The traditional layout is one of equal diamond shapes but you can work in squares, rectangles, or any geometric combination.

Upholstering is better done 'on the bench' rather than *in situ,* so first take out the panel/object to be covered and strip off all the existing trim. If you're dealing with a thin

hardboard panel, cut an identical shape out of ⅛ to ¼ inch (3 to 6mm) plywood or thicker for a stronger base.

Next, decide how you will fix the new panel within its area — to be easily removed in the future. There are various 'hidden fixing' clips on the market so check to see which type is best suited to your needs.

Now lay the panel on top of a sheet of foam (2 inch (5cm) thickness produces the best effect on most areas) and mark round the edges. Cut the foam exactly to shape and stick it to the face of the panel, using a recommended impact adhesive. For a nice cushioned edge to the finished work, carefully trim off a ½ inch (1.25cm) bevelled strip from the top edge of the foam with a sharp pair of shears. Alterna-

tively, you could cut the foam over size and staple the excess along the back edge of the panel. That is providing you allow for the subsequent extra width/length of the padded edges when cutting the panel to size in the first place.

Next draw up your pattern on paper, then transfer it to the foam. In traditional deep buttoning, the depth of each diamond is always greater than the width, and the straight pleats between the outer row of buttons and the edge of the panel slightly less than the diamond width (sides) and depth (top and bottom) where possible. If the panel shape is asymmetrical, keep the actual buttoning design symmetrical and balance the resultant pleat distances so that the whole thing looks right visually. This usually means leaving more space at the bottom than at the top.

Having marked up the pattern you can cut 1 inch (2.5cm) holes through the foam at the button location points. An electric drill fitted with a 1 inch (2.5cm) hole saw (with the centre pilot drill removed) is ideal for this purpose, providing you apply silicone spray to the actual saw. This will stop it catching the foam and help to produce a clean, cylindrical cut. An alternative is to heat up a length of 1 inch (2.5cm) diameter steel tube and press it slowly into the foam, using a slight circular motion. Wear asbestos gloves if you choose this method. You'll also need to drill a ⅛ inch (3mm) hole

Left: Buttons galore! This 'far from utilitarean' pick-up exploits a different technique known as float buttoning; where the buttons are pulled into the upholstered foam surface to form a neat pattern of hollows. Dralon is well suited as it reflects light, thus casting shadows. *Facing page:* Camaro interior sports deep buttoned, overhead luxury.

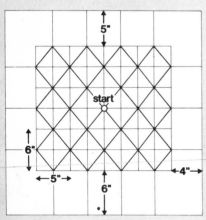

Example of pattern on foam

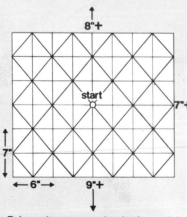

Enlarged pattern on back of material

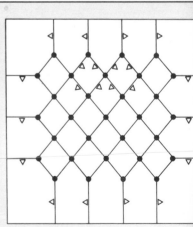

Directions of folds and pleats

hrough the plywood at the centre of each button recess for the buttoning needle to pass through easily.

You can now mark out the underside of your cover material to coincide with the foam pattern. You must allow for the extra material taken up in the pleated pockets. The distance between each button mark on the covering will usually increase by a distance equal to half the thickness of the foam. For example, if your pattern on 2 inch (5cm) foam includes diamonds that are 6 inches (15cms) deep and 5 inches (12.5cms) wide, the diamond size on the back of the material will increase by 1 inch (2.5cms) (depth and width) to 7 inches x 6 inches (17.5cms x 15cms). Draw up your enlarged pattern on paper, then transfer as before. Allow plenty of excess (3 or 4 inches (7.5 or 10cms)) all round the outer edges.

Before you proceed, you'll need a buttoning needle, twine and a supply of buttons covered in your chosen material. Buttons can be covered either by hand with a pair of pliers, or on a special button making machine. The latter is by far the easiest method, but unless you intend doing buttoning in a big way, a machine isn't really worth the outlay. Alternatively, you could try your local upholsterer.

Turn the panel so that the plywood is uppermost and insert two tacks either side of one ⅛ inch (3mm) hole, but without driving them fully into the wood. Take a length of twine, twist one end round one of the tacks and hammer it firmly into the wood. Repeat this process for each hole and turn the panel over. Whilst threading the buttons, you'll need to have access to both the top and underside, so it's a good idea to raise the panel off the ground by supporting it at either end (1).

Place a thin layer of wadding or similar over the foam so that it extends beyond the edges of the panel. Now lay your material on top and line up the centre button mark with the centre hole in the foam (2). Push the material into the hole as far as it will go, then turn your attention to the underside. Thread the loose end of the corresponding twine through the buttoning needle and push it up through the hole, foam and material (3). Unthread the twine and pass it through a button ring. Rethread and push the needle back to the underside. Draw up the twine, twist around the second tack and secure as before (4). Smooth the material/wadding away from the

anchored button and repeat the process for the next hole, making sure you place the marked spot accurately. Proceed diagonally outwards around the centre spot.

Do a few buttons then start to regulate the folds between them, using an upholsterers' regulator (5). If your measurements are accurate they will fall neatly into place, facing the bottom of the panel.

With all the buttons completed, start on the straight 'border' pleats. To achieve a consistent fullness, snip the wadding/foam from the outside button to the edge of the panel along the indicated pleat line, making the cut about ½ inch (1.25cm) deep (6). If the excess material/wadding exceeds 2 inches (5cms), trim it off square. Now fold the material under and tuck it into the foam (7). Pull it over the edge and tack the excess in place about 1 inch (2.5cms) inside the back edge of the panel (8). Do all the side pleats in the same manner.

For corner areas, first pull the centre back under the sides and tack in place (9). Lay the two side flaps over each other and fix to the plywood. Finish off by adding extra tacks for clean ridge-free edges.

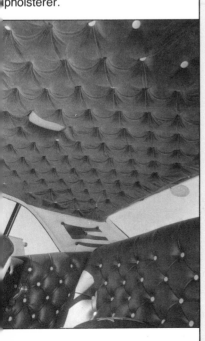

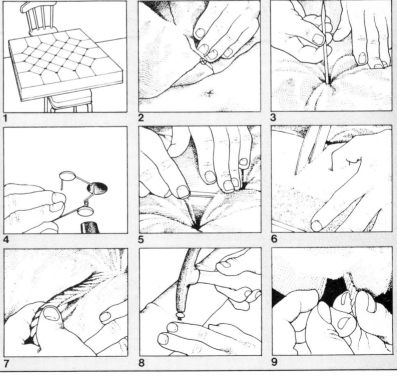

Tuck'n'roll

If you're out to create a fifties style custom, a tuck'n'roll interior should be high on your list of priorities. It consists of neatly padded channels of material and is, traditionally, the favourite amongst customizers. The style can look equally effective when applied in low-key, resto-rod moderation or as an all out extreme attack — typified by many of the early sixties show cars that incorporated tuck'n'rolled trunks, hoods and wheelwells!

To achieve the parallel rolls or 'flutes', it is essential that you are able to machine-sew a perfectly straight line. Distorted pleats will ruin the overall effect, so practise first on old sheets or similar.

Apart from your chosen cover material (leather, leathercloths and vinyls are best suited), you'll need some calico as undercovering and a suitable material for stuffing the flutes, such as wadding or lintafelt. Basically, the process involves marking up the intended flute width lines on the calico, similar but oversize lines on the cover, and stitching the two together. The channels are then stuffed to produce a firm, even wave form to the material.

Taking the top of a bench seat as a classic example of tuck'n'roll appli-cation, the first thing to do, as always, is transfer the item from car to bench and carefully remove the existing trim. Measure the area/old cover from top to bottom, add on at least 4 inches (10cms) 'safety excess' and note the minimum width of material/calico required. Now measure the seat from side to side and decide what width of flute you want (normally about 1½ to 2 inches (4 to 5cms)). You can then calculate the total number of flutes by dividing the length of seat measurement by the flute width. If it doesn't work out to a round figure, the extra can be added to the outside flutes for correct visual balance. The total length of calico required will equal the length of the seat, plus the usual 4 inches (10cms) for safety. However, you must allow an extra ½ inch (12mm) per flute on the cover material for stitching and fullness.

The next stage requires a high degree of accuracy in marking out these measurements on the materials (see diagram). Lay the materials flat and smooth on the bench and make certain that the parallel flute lines are perfectly square to the outer edges. It's also a good idea to number them from left to right on the calico, and right to left on the underside of the cover material, to avoid confusion when stitching.

If the cover is a leather/leather-cloth type of material, it must be creased initially to enable straighter and easier machining. Starting at one end, fold along the first flute line so that the line is still visible. Using the handle of a pair of shears, rub the fold with pressure (1) so that the crease shows on the other side (face side). Repeat along each line until the piece is finished.

Lay the calico so that the first flute line on the left (number one) is under the foot of the sewing machine, and the rest of this material lies to the right. Now place the first creased line of the cover material (number one) on top, so that the two lines abut and the remainder lies to the left. You can then machine a per-fectly straight seam (tuck), ⅛ inch (3mm) inside and parallel to the line(s) through both thicknesses (2). Move the calico across, fold (roll) to the next line and stitch as before (3). Continue to tuck'n'roll to the end.

For permanent shape the rolls need padding with suitably sized strips of wadding. Each strip must be identical in width and thickness

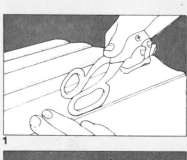

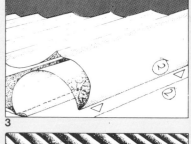

Diagram shows basic principle for marking out calico and cover material. The required width flutes are marked on the calico and the lines numbered from left to right. The same number of flutes are marked on the cover, but you must allow an extra ½ inch (12mm) width on each one. Dotted lines indicate safety excess, at least 2½ inches (6.25cms) all round.

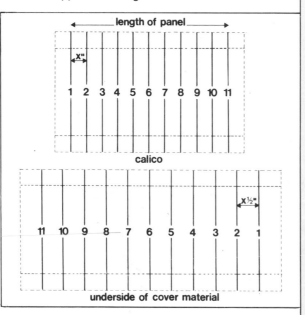

length of panel

X"

1 2 3 4 5 6 7 8 9 10 11

calico

X½"

11 10 9 8 7 6 5 4 3 2 1

underside of cover material

for a uniform finish, so take care if cutting your own. A better idea for standard sized flutes is to buy your wadding ready-cut to the correct width. To distribute the padding, take two long, thin strips of sheet plastic, place your padding between the two and tie the 'sandwich' at one end with a piece of fabric. Insert this end into the open roll and push gently until it protrudes at the other end (4). Untie the fabric, pull out the plastic strips and trim off the excess for an even distribution of padding.

You can now trim the fluted material to fit the proposed area. In the case of a top panel on a bench seat, first locate the material centrally and squarely on the padded seat base. Now mark the outer edges of the seat on the material (5). Remove the material, place it under the sewing machine and stich along the marked line (6), then cut off the excess about 2 inches (5cms) ahead of the seam. The new top panel will then be ready for joining to the lower panel(s), which should include at least 3 inches (7.5cms) excess.

Piping

The usual method of joining one upholstered panel to another, whilst simultaneously concealing the outer seam, is to use piping. It is made by covering a length of nylon cord with your chosen cover material, possibly in a contrasting colour.

Measure the seams to be piped for the total length of cord/material required. Cut the material in strip(s) about 2 inches (5cms) wide and lay the cord down the centre of the underside. Fold the two edges together and seam as close to the cord as possible without sewing into it, making sure that the cord is tightly covered.

With the nylon cord sewn in, the piping can be sandwiched between the two edges of the panels. This involves straightforward aligning of the two panels under the machine, and also the positioning of the piping so that it covers the previously sewn edging stitches. First 'tack stitch' the material in position by hand, then machine through all thicknesses just below the piping (using a special piping 'foot'). This will result in a neat, attractive edge where the seam is undetectable.

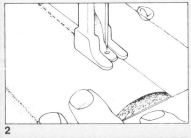

2

4

6

Right: Exterior theme carried through to the interior of Ford Pop, entitled 'Soul Sensation'.
Far right: 1970 Austin pick-up lends itself well to traditional 50's custom interior treatment.

Right and far right: Today's street machines are built to look as good as they perform, as proven by the slick, up-dated upholstering of the beautiful '55 Chevys.
Below: A classic example of imaginative tuck'n' roll using contrasting coloured flutes. In terms of pure nostalgia, this style takes a lot of beating.

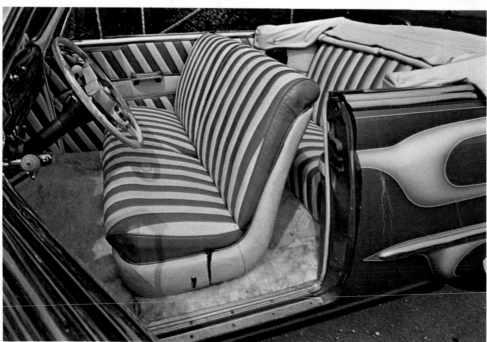

Right: It's amazing what can be done to a seat, given enough creative thought.
Far right: Tasteful use of natural materials and colour accentuates the 'genuine' feel of this Model 'A' roadster.

Right: Inviting interior of this late model lowridin' sedan is trimmed in tuck'n'rolled crushed velvet with contrasting inserts/piping.

Right: Radical engine swop means recessed bulkhead which, in turn, equals one 'back seat driver'. Note cockpit-style aluminium dash arrangement.

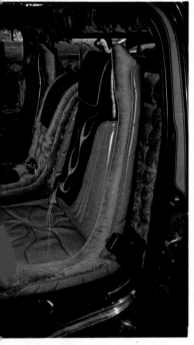

Dashboards et cetera

Unless you're building a very authentic resto-rod, the chances are that you'll either want to modify the existing dashboard/instrumentation, or otherwise remove/panel over it completely. There are literally countless possibilities in this direction, especially if you choose to start from scratch. This will allow you to design a new arrangement, free of factory restrictions and tailored exactly to your practical and aesthetic needs.

The best material to use, if you want plenty of curves on your new dash, is fibre glass, 'layed up' from a female mould of hand carved polyurethane foam. The latter cuts easily with a sharp knife and can be sanded smooth with sandpaper. Plywood or sheet aluminium are fine for constructing flat edged shapes.

If the original dash was covered so as to appear as a blank panel it could be painted (possibly with small murals or pinstriping), or upholstered to match the rest of your interior. Secondary instruments could be mounted in an overhead console made from plywood, while the important ones could be mounted in a centre console or housed within a visible hood scoop.

As an alternative, you could mount all your gauges behind a slightly tinted perspex panel so as not to be seen, but lit up from behind when the ignition is turned on.

Pedals also offer a lot of room for creativity. You can make your own individual shapes, or words, e.g. GAS, STOP, by cutting and filing steel plate then plating with chrome, brass, silver or copper. The same goes for steering wheels, incorporating almost any centre pattern/rim shape you wish. It's really all down to your imagination!

Above: Large diameter steering wheel adds to the vintage look.
Left: Ford Pop incorporates pile covered custom dash, housing full Jaguar instrumentation.
Right: Exterior lettering on this Corvette street racer reads 'THE EXECUTIONER'.

Ready to Cruise

'Do it, do it'! 'Lay rubber, man'! 'Smoke them tyres'! — familiar cat calls from many a crowded American side-walk on a Saturday night. That is, when the street machiners are out there creating a stir on the main drag. Spirits are high and everybody's out for a good time. Stockers roll by unnoticed. Suddenly, a loud cheer goes up as the local 'big block' hero brings the traffic to a standstill. Frantic action follows.

Young guys flood onto the street and surround the car. Water and beer are thrown over the tyres. Girlish screams of 'Hey Scott, c'mon Scott'! are soon muted as he winds up the roarin' motor. Screechin' tyres deafen the smoke-filled atmosphere. He holds it for a full twenty seconds, then burns out in a snake path to the stop light. The crowd go wild with excitement and plead for more action. Tyre smokin' street action.

Every year thousands of rods from all over the United States congregate for the biggest event of them all — the NSRA Street Rod Nationals. 1979 marked its tenth anniversary, held in St. Paul, Minnesota. For four days and nights this mid-west town was dominated by all types of pre '49 machinery, enthusiasts and spectators. Parading, admiring, polishing and cruising. The Nats are a whole lotta fun!

Facing page: Local highways become a rolling rod show throughout the day and most of the night. *Left:* Fun, fun, crazy fun! *Centre:* Young girl looking after the pride of the family, for which the event involved a 4000 mile round-trip. *Below:* Both spectators and admirers had a great time.

Right: An overall view of the NSRA Street Machine Nationals, Milwaukee '79. *Below:* Evil, wicked, mean 'n' nasty. *Facing page, top left:* Total performance? *Top right:* The fun's in the run! *Centre right:* Two rods rump-rumping it at the stop-light. *Below:* Caught in the act of duty.

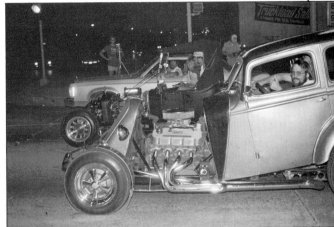

Glossary of Terms

The colourful spirit of the custom scene would be incomplete without a jargon all of its own. Definitions such as 'a blown goat' or a 'super-sano panel' say as much about the individual nature of the subject as the cars themselves. Listed below are a number of references commonly used by customizers.

A

Air-shocks
Adjustable shock absorbers which can be pumped up, enabling an increase or decrease in the ride height.

Appletons
Small spotlights mounted at the base of windshield pillars. Used purely for show on fifties style customs, they are invariably turned down facing the body to give a more streamlined appearance.

B

Barris
George Barris, the most influential American customizer. Renowned for the creation of many classic customs during the fifties and sixties.

Beef
To strengthen. Usually applied to chassis or suspension work.

Big 'n' littles
The classic street rod combination of fat rear wheels along with smaller, skinny ones at the front.

Blower
Custom slang for a supercharger, which serves to pressurise the mixture of petrol and air into the engine.

Boots
Tyres, e.g. big boots means fat tyres.

Bug catcher
Metal scoop mounted on top of the carburetter(s), that functions as a direct air intake.

C

Carson top
A low, deeply padded soft top for convertibles. Manufactured by the Carson Top Company during the fifties and sixties.

C-cab
Type of street rod, so called because of the C-shaped cab opening. Design was derived from early commercial cab units.

Channelling
A method of reducing the overall height of a car. Involves cutting the floor loose from the body sides, dropping the body by the desired amount, then re-welding the floor back in, consequently reducing interior height as well.

Chopping
Lowering the roofline of a car by cutting the desired amount out of the roof and door pillars, then welding the sections back together again. Easily performed on early cars that have a vertical structure, where re-alignment and glass cutting present few problems.

Chromies
Short for chrome reversed rim wheels. A set of chromies were the mark of an authentic rod or custom before the advent of mag wheels.

Continental kit
Very fashionable, high status symbol during the early fifties. It consisted of a spare wheel mounted in all its glory on a step on the rear bumper.

D

Dagmars
Chromed features, mounted onto bumpers on cars of the fifties. Purely for show, their abstract implications led to them being named after a certain voluptuous film actress.

De-chroming
Cleaning up the lines of a car by removing all the unnecessary chrome protuberances, whilst simultaneously taking away the identifiable 'factory look'.

De-seaming
The process of filling in the seams between abutting panels in order to give a smoother, one-piece appearance.

Deuce Coupe
A two-seater closed coupe produced by Henry Ford in 1932. One of the classic designs of street rodding, as depicted in the film *American Graffiti,* and in the lyrics of the Beach Boys' hit record, *Little Deuce Coupe.*

Dual-gate shifter
A dual pattern gear shifter, enabling either automatic or manual changing of gears. Often custom-made for a unique effect.

E

Etching
The process of decorating glass either by sand-blasting or brushing an acid-based cream over a masked design.

F

Fad 'T'
Radical version of Model 'T' street rod. Improvisation includes a shorter than normal wheelbase, big 'n' littles, and a steep hood to accentuate the forward rake.

Fenderskirts
Metal attachments that are clipped over the rear wheelwells. By concealing most of the wheel and tyre, they help to give a longer, lower, overall appearance. Standard wear on most early customs.

Flares
Wheelwells that are stretched outward in order to accommodate larger wheels and tyres. Achieved by adding glass fibre attachments or fabricating with metal.

Flathead
An engine in which the valves are mounted alongside the cylinders, not in the cylinder head.

Fleetside
A pick-up truck, on which the vertical sides of the rear bed run flush with the cab doors.

Flip front
A one-piece front end that can be hinged forward, allowing maximum access to the engine.

Flippers
Chromed wheel trims that have a raised criss-cross pattern on a slightly hollow face. Typically ostentatious feature of the fifties custom.

Four by four (4X4)
A vehicle that incorporates four wheel drive in order to withstand rugged off-road use.

Four on the floor
Another name for a floor mounted, four speed manual gear change.

Frenching
Most commonly used to describe the recessing of lights or aerials into the body. The term also applies to the joining of a trim piece, such as a headlight or tail-light rim to the adjoining body panel.

Fuzzy dice
Hung from the rear view mirror, they were initially symbolic of the way in which the hot rodder spent his life, 'dicing with death'.

G

Goat
The pontiac GTO. One of America's classic 'muscle cars', first produced in 1964.

GRP
Glass-reinforced plastic, more commonly known as glass fibre. Light, non-corrosive material from which such things as flares, air damns, scoops and even complete auto bodies are constructed.

H

Hemi
An engine with a hemispherical (highly efficient) combustion chamber. Normally found in 'speed' cars and dragsters.

Hi-boy
A term used to describe a fender-less roadster that incorporates a slightly higher-than-normal ground clearance.

Hi-rider
A car that is jacked up all round for the true street-racer look.

Hop-up
Synonymous with engine tweak. Also a popular U.S. enthusiast magazine that evolved in the mid-fifties.

Hot rod
The original term for what is now known as a street rod. A typical post-war hot rod was chopped, fenderless, highly tuned and, of course, flamed.

I

Injectors
A fuel injection system which squirts precisely metered quantities of fuel into the inlet ports.

IRS
Independent rear suspension. A set-up whereby each rear wheel has a separate linkage to the chassis, allowing it to move up or down without influencing the other. Normally exposed and chromed for a dazzling effect beneath the rear end of a street rod.

J

Jimmy blower
A supercharger originally designed for GMC trucks, that soon became popular amongst hot rodders.

K

Kings Road
Famous road in West London, where customizers display their machines on the last Saturday of each month.

Knobbies
Chunky treaded tyres designed for off-road use.

Kustom City
The most prolific and influential customizing shop of the post-war period, run by George Barris and his late brother Sam.

L

Lakes pipes
Narrow chromed sidepipes that run beneath the rocker panels and help to give a lower, more stream-lined appearance.

Leadsled
A term used to describe many early customs, some of which carried up to 100-lbs. (45-kgs.) extra weight in lead filler after chopping, de-seaming, frenching, etc.

Louvres
Series of small slots pressed into metal for ventilation purposes. Usually incorporated within the hood to let hot air out or cool air in.

Low-boy
A channelled, fenderless Ford roadster.

Lowrider
A car that has been radically lowered, normally for 'show' rather than 'go'. Although the term can be applied to many early customs, it is usually associated with a conspicuous Californian automotive sub-culture.

m

Mill
Engine.

Mini truck
A small contemporary pick-up truck.

Moon discs
Spun aluminium discs that conceal the entire wheel. Originally designed to cut down wind resistance in high-speed machinery.

N,O

Nerf bars
Simple unobtrusive substitute for bumpers. Normally custom-made from steel tubing, then chromium plated.

Nose and decking
Removing all factory ornamenta-tion from the hood and deck lid and filling the holes for a smooth appearance.

Opera windows
Small windows, mounted within rear roof pillars or panelled-in side windows.

P,Q

Pancaked hood
A hood which, instead of being deeply crowned, has been re-shaped or fabricated to a flat shape.

Phone booth
An apt name given to a particular type of Model 'T' Ford which has a tall two-seater cab.

Quick-change rear
A final drive arrangement, whereby the rear axle ratio can be quickly changed either for normal street use or racing.

R

Radiusing
Enlarging or opening-up of wheel-wells for practical or aesthetic reasons.

Rag top
Custom slang for a convertible.

Repro-rod
A GRP-bodied street rod of which there are numerous types on the market, such as the Ford Models 'A', 'B' and 'T'.

Roadster
An open top vehicle in which passengers ride totally exposed to the elements.

Rumble seat
Additional seat situated in the trunk, where an open deck lid serves as back support. A common feature in many early roadsters.

RV
Abbreviation of recreational vehicle. Mini trucks, campers, buggies etc. all fall within this category.

S

Scallops
Wild paint design in which U-shaped patterns extend and taper to fine points.

Sectioning
Difficult operation that involves removing a uniform horizontal strip of metal from a car's body. The upper and lower halves of the body are then welded back together, producing a lean, low-profile look.

Sedan delivery
A small utility vehicle, similar to a shooting brake with the side rear windows and doors panelled-in.

Slush box
Automatic gearbox.

Spoiler
Air dam mounted beneath the front valence and/or deck lid of a car to aid stability at high speeds.

Stepside
A type of mini truck, that incorporates abbreviated running boards between the back of the cab and bulbous rear fenders.

Stocker
Any standard factory-built car. The age old saying, 'only your mother drives a stocker' clarifies this further.

Straight tube axle
Recognisable feature on many high riding street machines. The front axle takes the form of a straight tube, onto which leaf springs are mounted in order to raise the car's height.

Street machine
A rather loose definition that can be applied to almost any 'personalised car' built in or after 1949, whether for speed, style or both.

Street rod
Strictly speaking, a specialist machine based on any vehicle that was originally constructed before 1949. However, the term is often applied more loosely to any 'early looking' customized car in countries outside the U.S.A.

Street sleeper
A car which, under a deceivingly straight exterior, has been extensively modified for increased performance.

Stretching
The extension or re-shaping of any body panel for whatever reason. For example, fenders are often lengthened (stretched) to enhance the profile of a car.

Suicide doors
Doors that are hinged on the opposite side to the present-day type and therefore swing open from the front as opposed to the rear.

Super-sano
Describes a car that is 'sanitary' clean in all departments, i.e. body, interior, engine bay etc.

Swallowtail doors
Doors on a roadster or convertible, that are cut down along their top edge, usually on a taper towards the rear to give a more 'open' appearance to a car.

T

T-bucket
Very popular open two-seater street rod, based on Henry Ford's biggest seller — the Model 'T'.

Three on the tree
A term used to describe a three speed gear change mounted on the steering column.

Tin
Old production car with an appearance and construction that lends itself to custom treatment.

Tube grille
Custom radiator grille, made up from lengths of chromed tubing.

Tuck 'n' roll
Traditional upholstery style for the custom interior. The material, usually naugahyde, is tucked under and rolled back before stitching.

Turbo
Short for turbocharger, which is a type of supercharger driven by the energy in the exhaust gases instead of mechanically from the crankshaft.

U,V

Ute
A factory-built pick-up which is based on a normal passenger car.

Van Nuys
Famous cruising area for street rods and customs, situated just north of Los Angeles.

Vette
Pet name for the ever popular Chevrolet Corvette.

Vicky
The name given to a particular style of 1930s sedan that incorporates a gently curved rear end.

W

Wide whites
Tyres that have a broad white sidewall band. Very symbolic of the fifties when they were fitted as standard wear on most factory-built cars.

Woody
A shooting brake that incorporates a structural wooden framework and side panelling. Fashionable amongst the sixties surfing set in the U.S.A.

Z

Z-ing
Method of lowering the ride height of a car by re-locating the chassis rails over the rear axle.

Zoomies
Exhaust pipes that are angled in an upright direction.

Appendix

A & L Autos,
96 North Street, Romford, Essex.
(Custom Paint Supplies)

Alexander Engineering Co. Ltd.,
Haddeham, Aylesbury,
Bucks. HP17 8BZ

American Auto Spares,
91 Moyser Road, Streatham,
London SW16.

American Tyre Sales,
31/33 Fortune Green Road,
London, NW6.

Americar,
352/354 Southchurch Road,
Southend-on-Sea, Essex.

Anglo American Autoparts,
Seven Oaks Crescent,
Bramcote, Nottingham.

Autocraft Custom,
Gate Cottage, Bolnhurst, Beds.

Auto Imagination,
Foxton Mews,
48 Friars Stile Road,
Richmond Hill, Surrey.

Autoquip Custom Centre,
110 Hagley Road West,
Warley, West Midlands. B67 5EZ.

Baja (Four Wheel Drive),
The Mews, Ravens Croft Road,
Henley-on-Thames, Oxon.

Big J Autoparts,
Dept. D. Unicorn House, Lake Street,
Leighton Buzzard, Beds.
(Warehouse & Distribution Centre)

Also at:
46 Camden High Street,
London, NW1.

British Oxygen Company Ltd.,
Dawson Road, Bletchley,
Milton Keynes.
(Welding Equipment)

John Brown Wheels Ltd.,
Wedgock Lane, Warwick, CV34 5YA.
(Mail Order Dept.)

Budget Racing,
York Road, Ilford, Essex.

Cal Brook Cars,
Commerce Estate, Kingston Road,
Leatherhead, Surrey.
(Custom Paint Supplies)

Causeway Auto Services,
321 Lodge, Causeway,
Fishponds, Bristol.

Cobra Automotive Products Ltd.,
Heslop, Halesfield 23, Telford.
(Wheels)

Connoisseur Car Books,
28 Devonshire Road,
Chiswick, London W4.

Creech Coach Trimming Centre,
67 High Street, South Norwood,
London, SE25 6EB.
Also at:
45 Anerley Road, Penge,
London SE.

Cruiser Van Co. Ltd.,
1 Gammons Lane,
Watford, Herts., WD2 5BZ.

Custom Maid,
323 High Road, Ilford, Essex.

Custom Performance,
Church Lane, Clowne,
Chesterfield, S43 4AZ.

Customville,
859 High Road, Goodmayes, Essex.

Deals-on-Wheels,
57 London Road,
Southend-on-Sea,
Essex.

Dees Custom Shop.
Birkenhead Market, Merseyside.

DMC,
North Road, Okehampton,
Devon, EX20 1BQ.
(Custom Glass Fibre)

East Coast Speed and Custom Shop,
24 Cyprus Street, Norwich, Norfolk.

Fibresports,
34/36 Bowlers Croft,
No. 1 Industrial Estate,
Basildon, Essex.

Gable Arc Welders Ltd.,
Cattle Market, Hereford.

Gary's Shack,
62 Battersea High Street,
London, SW11.
(American Specialists)

B.F. Goodrich,
257/259 Portland Road,
South Norwood, London, SE25.
(Mail Order Only)

Howley Racing,
Winnick Road, Warrington, WAZ 7PA.

Jeff Howe Exhausts,
Main Road (A20),
West Kingsdown, Kent.

Geoff Jago Custom Automotive,
Quarry Lane, Chichester, Sussex.

Kens Custom Car Centre,
168 Fawcett Road,
Southsea, Hants.

Mech-Spray,
11/16 Miles Place, Deluce Road,
Rochester, Kent.

Metalflake Distributors,
Commerce Estate, 69 Kingston Road,
Leatherhead, Surrey.

Mini Sport,
Thompson Street, Padiham, Lancs.

Harry Moss International Ltd.,
Hemming Road,
Washford Industrial Estate,
Redditch, Worcs.

Muscle City,
678 Pershore Road,
Selly Park, Birmingham.

Quality Rod Parts PWC Ltd.,
Maple Works Unit 2,
Old Shoreham Road, Hove,
East Sussex, BN3 7EX.

Quip Accessories,
Halifax Road, Drewsbury,
West Yorks., WF13 4AW.

Rod & Custom Shop,
226 Stockport Road,
Cheadleheath, Manchester.

Rolling Stock,
826 Wickham Road,
Shirley, Croydon, Surrey.

Sperex,
College Street, Kempston, Bradford.

Street Dreams,
98 Wellington Street,
Luton, Beds.

Street Rod Engineering,
26 Hockerill Street,
Bishops Stortford, Herts.

A.G.Thorpe (Development),
60 Wellington Street, Derby.
(Body Custom Kits)

The Van Shop GB.,
341/345 Roman Road,
London, E3.

West Coast Customs,
65/69 College Road,
Crosby, Liverpool, 23.

Wheelspin Custom,
51 York Street, Twickenham, Middx.

Wolfrace Equipment,
Elms Industrial Estate,
Shuttleworth Road,
Goldington, Bedford.
(Head Office & Mail Order)

Aero-Lac Automotive Finishes,
SEM Products, Inc.,
Sem Lane & Shoreway Road,
Belmont, California 94002.

Automotive Accessories Unlimited,
2609 Woodland, Anaheim,
California 92801.

Auto World, Inc.,
701 N. Keyser Avenue, Scranton,
Pennsylvania 18508.

Avi Naftel, Avi's Custom Creations,
160 North Baldwin Street,
Johnson City, New York.

Badger Airbrush Co.,
9201 Gage Avenue, Franklin Park,
Illinois 60131.

Barris Kustom Industries,
10811 Riverside Drive, N. Hollywood,
California 91602.

Bits & Pieces,
3201 Telegraph Avenue, Oakland,
California.

California Step Side, Inc.,
P.O.Box 60249, Sunnyvale,
California 94088.

Carl Green Enterprises.
7749 Densmore Avenue # 7,
Van Nuys, California 91406.

Coleman Bros. Speed Shop,
7443 Washington Blvd., Baltimore,
Maryland.

Color Man,
1713 N. Orange Thorpe Park, Anaheim,
California 92801.

The Crazy Painters,
9665 Alondra Blvd., Bellflower,
California 90706.

Dan Woods Ent.,
15516 Vermont Avenue, Paramount,
California 90723.

Dean Jeffries' Automotive Styling,
3077 No. Cahegua Avenue,
Hollywood, California 90068.

Dick Dean Auto Reconstruction,
6920-D Knott Avenue, Beuna Park,
California 90620.

Far Performance Inc.,
1931 Old Middlefield Way,
Mountain View, California 94040,

The Frame Shop,
7220 Alabama Avenue, Canoga Park,
California 91303.

Genuine Suspension,
1361 E. Pomona, Santa Ana,
California 92705.

Hickey Enterprises,
1645 Callens Road, Ventura,
California 93003.

Hi Enterprises,
11709 Cardinal Circle,
Garden Grove,
California 92643.

Hi Rev,
215 East 29th Street, Marshfield,
Wisconsin.

Joe Bailon,
5955 Troost Avenue, N. Hollywood,
California 91607.

Low Manufacturing,
245 W. Foothill Blvd., Monrovia,
California 91016.

Mag Buff,
3008 S. Orange, Santa Ana,
California 92627.

Motion Performance Parts, Inc.,
598 Sunrise Highway, Baldwin, L.I.,
New York 11510.

Nationwise Rod Shop,
P.O.Box 27168, Columbus,
Ohio 43227.

Pacer Performance,
5345 San Fernando Road West,
Los Angeles, California 90039.

Pete & Jakes,
8827 E. Las Tunas Drive,
Temple City, California 91780.

Salem Off-Road Center,
2715 Portland Road, N.E., Salem,
Oregon.

Steve's Paint'n Place,
17452 Clark Avenue, Bell Flower,
California 90706.

Stewart-Warner Corp.,
1826 Diverse Parkway,
Chicago, Illinois 60614.

Street Customs Ltd.,
11737 Cardinal Circle, Garden Grove,
California 92643.

Today's World Interiors,
3521 Tweedy Blvd., South Gate,
California 90820.

Total Performance Inc.,
406 South Orchard Street,
Route 5, Wallingford, CT. 06492.

Traditional Street Rods,
P.O. Box 8186, La Crescenta,
California 91214.

4 x 4 & Van Center Ltd.,
967 Thayer Avenue, Silver Spring,
Maryland.

Whitlock Performance Center,
10130 West Appleton Avenue,
Milwaukee, Wisconsin.

Wilcap Company,
2930 Sepulveda Blvd., Torrance,
California 90510.

Winfield Special Products,
7749 Densmore Avenue, # 6,
Van Nuys, California 91406.

Z-Place,
19735 Sherman Way, Unit # 1,
Canoga Park, California 91306.

Bibliography

Arco Publishing Co. Inc.
Customizing Vans

Auto Media
Complete Guide to American Cars
1966—76

Badger
Airbrushing Techniques

HP Books
How to Rebuild S/Black Ford (V8)
How to Rebuild S/Block Chevy
Turbochargers
How to Hot Rod S/Block Chevy
How to Hot Rod VW Engines
Holley Carbs & Manifolds
Clutch & Flywheel Handbook
Baja — Prepping VW Sedans & Buggys

Kona Publications Ltd.
The Big Dummy's Guide to CB Radio

Metalflake
Art of Custom Painting

Petersen Publishing Co.
Custom Painting
Rod and Custom
Vans
Pick-ups & Mini Trucks
Street Freaks
Street Machines and Bracket Racing
Engines No. 2
Chevy Hi-Performance
How to Build a Street Rod
Creative Customising
Pick-Ups & Vans
Basic Bodywork & Painting No. 4
Complete Four-Wheel-Drive

SA Design
Superpower Guide to Nitrous etc.
Mopar Performance
Ford Performance
Bolt-on Performance

Frederick Warne
American Cars of the 60's
American Cars of the 50's
American Cars of the 30's